ISBN-13: 978-1508717546 (Paperback)

ISBN-10: 1508717540   (eBook)

Available on Amazon

*to Li
Love is all there is
Patricia* ♡

Published in Canada by

DCL

Suite 226

9049 Commercial Street

New Minas NS B4N 5A4

This is What Love Looks Like, Too

Dr. Patricia P. Grover Dix

IN MEMORIAM

This book is dedicated to my dear best male friend, **Dennis Campbell**, who passed into

his energetic state suddenly one day before his birthday in October, 2014.

THANK YOU

Thank you to all the learning opportunities I have had in my life – so far – to learn about the power of LOVE.

Thank you to Jerusha for proofreading.

Thank you to Karen for continual support.

Thank you to all those who showed excitement and urged me on when I talked about the project of writing this book.

Thank you to Alex for suggesting the workbook format.

Thank you, especially to all the people and animal friends for their stories shared here; this book would not exist without them.

Thank you to the Divine for everything I have been gifted with in my life. I am truly blessed.

IN THE BEGINNING, NOW, and FOREVER MORE...there is LOVE.

> **LOVE** is like a snowflake: one perfect exquisite snowflake melts, barely leaving a trace. Add billions of snowflakes to the one and there is a winter wonderland.
> **LOVE** is like a blade of grass: one day there is brown earth, a few days following and there are pale green grass shoots. Without their growth being perceptible, the blades of grass continue to grow greener and greener – ever so imperceptibly.
> **LOVE** is like a rain drop. One drop isn't noticed; however, when millions of raindrops coalesce, there is now a stream, now a river, and, now an ocean.
> **LOVE** is like the wind: it cannot be seen – only the results of its action are visible for all to see.

Do you recognize and honour Love as it happens in your life? Every day? Every minute? Can you recognize Love in its vagaries and varieties and hues and shades: the colour, taste, smell, sound, sight of Love – or is it only a feeling that you recognize? It might surprise you to realize that we all want Love, talk about it, search for it, dream of it, yet, we so often fail to recognize it when we are graced with its presence. **LOVE**, you see, IS all there is. It is the blue of the sky, the green of the grass, the brown of the earth, the white of the snowflake, the translucent reflective silver of the raindrop, and the effects of the wind – **LOVE** is and Is and IS.

Most of my life I spent afraid. I now know that there are only two choices in life: LOVE or FEAR. These two choices come in many different guises. A sample of the variations for these two choices follows.

FEAR also known as:		LOVE also known as:	
anger	criticism	joy	bliss
revenge	unforgiveness	passion	laughter
depression	lack of self-worth	grins	self-worth
non-acceptance	ungratefulness	acceptance	forgiveness
past	future	gratefulness	thankfulness
guilt	shame	happiness	present now
lonely	sadness	ecstasy	pleasure
doom	grief	elation	hopefulness
anxiety	panic	helpfulness	powerfulness
resentment	jealousy	anticipation	courage
fatigue	tension	desire	love
boredom	withdrawal	interest	wonder
worry	neglect	surprise	elation
abandonment	disgust	choice	liking
afraid	embarrassment	caring	compassion
regret	envy	adoration	affection
helplessness	hopelessness	tenderness	sentimentality

powerlessness	judgmental	cheerfulness	glee
aversion	dejection	delight	gladness
hate	despair	enjoyment	euphoria
rage	terror	zest	enthusiasm
contempt	pain	thrill	excitement
pessimism	hostility	eagerness	optimism
bitterness	spite	rapture	amazement
scorn	suffering	astonishment	pity
isolation	alienation	sympathy	enthralled
neglect	rejection	eagerness	zeal
defeat	insecurity	satisfaction	cheerfulness
tenseness	dread	jolliness	pride
distress	uneasiness	resiliency	empathy
homesickness	humiliation	trusting	awe
insult	remorse	calm	serene
torment	greed	relaxed	friendliness
gluttony	sloth	boldness	contentment
lust	contempt	curiosity	fearlessness
unsupported	destructive	interested	pleasure
aggressive	passive	energetic	kind
hostile	grumpy	warm-hearted	soft
wrath	angst	concerned	creative
apathy	shyness	inspired	fervor
jittery	terrified	sensitiveness	motivated
irritated	fearful		

At its basic level of utility, Fear tells us that something is amiss. Maybe we are in physical, emotional, or spiritual danger. Fear is an emotion to be reckoned with. It has its purpose in our lives; however, when Fear becomes entrenched as a way of thinking, acting, believing, then it blocks our souls from their intended paths. As you might feel from the above list of Fear-based states of consciousness, they all vibrate at slow levels. Who wants to be vibrating slowly like a slug? After one assesses a situation where Fear has arisen and found it wanting in terms of survival, then one's ego is what stands to gain from keeping us in this state. Ego versus higher consciousness or as some call it, God-consciousness. There really is no choice here. Actively being aware of our thoughts on a continual basis, challenging those that are fear-based, making us feel 'less than' must be rooted out and replaced with more life-affirming thoughts because these then become the attractors to bring more life-affirming actions and experiences into our lives. The Bible says that we get back what we sow at least threefold. Some say it is tenfold. Whatever the detail, I would think we would want more of the good stuff and less of the stuff that makes us feel shamed, guilt-ridden, less than, rejected, neglected, and not accepted. We have the power to change our thinking which then changes what we manifest in our lives on a daily basis. Look Fear in the eye when he comes bidding and do a critical assessment of whether it is ego talking about keeping the status quo of your little life and little self – or should it be replaced with an alternative life-enhancing, love-attracting attitude and belief system. As Einstein said, "Insanity is *doing the same thing* over and over again and expecting different results." Thinking we are each responsible for all our thoughts and actions begins the transformation of taking back our power, learning that control is an illusion and giving ourselves permission to be guided by our higher selves, regardless of the outcomes, is always in our highest good. Any and all experiences are always for our highest good. They are our lessons. Our lessons about LOVE. That is why we came here – to learn about LOVE.

Never underestimate the cunningness of irrational Fear. It can be addictive, especially to a heart that has not had enough LOVE experiences to be able to compare. This addictive nature of Fear also releases endorphins into our blood stream giving us that 'feel good' feeling. Trying to suppress or negate our feelings of Fear does not get rid of them, it just lets them hide and come out in inappropriate ways at inappropriate times in our lives. We must face our Fear, as the saying goes. Take it out, examine it, see if it has validity, LOVE it. Yes, I said LOVE it. LOVE our fears.

From the above list, you can quickly see that each emotion is like looking at a coin, one side, then the other side. Fear and LOVE are the two sides of the same coin. To negate one loses the other, too. Therefore, LOVE your Fear, breathe in to it, LOVE it into transforming it into its counterpart – LOVE made up of kindness, compassion, joy, bliss, peace. Once we accept Fear for its role in our lives, we can then look on it with compassion. And, once we let go of allowing Fear to run our lives, then LOVE in all its manifestations has room to expand in an outward spiral, touching all in our sphere of cognition and influence.

People who live in Fear are reluctant participants in the human experience – the most difficult choice a soul can have. That reluctant human syndrome of living a life based on Fear, of not being in a safe place, has its roots that were laid down in the brain while that soul was in the womb, at delivery, or in the first three years of birth. There are some who would say that we could also bring past life karma with us to be resolved in this lifetime, and Fear could manifest itself through this channel, too. As *A Course in Miracles* says, "Miracles are natural. When they do not occur, something has gone wrong. I believe that the 'something' that prevents miracles from freely occurring is our uptight attitudes and fear. When you affirm, "This situation is already healed, right now," the words' soothing effects lift fear long enough for miracles to occur naturally."

Fear notifies us that something significant is going to happen in our lives. It is a signal that we are moving from a familiar situation to one with new possibilities, untried experiences, unknown results. This can be unsettling. It can also be exhilarating. We need to honour our Fears as the harbingers of change that they are. They call us to become aware, pay attention to our intention, get ready, change is coming. Since thoughts become the basis for our energy's state at any point in time, monitoring our thoughts allows us to become the masters of our own destinies. Our thoughts become our deeds which become our reality manifested in physical form. We become the dreamer and the dream within the web of life all at the same time.

I also know that if one chooses LOVE, then Fear is not an option. One cannot jointly choose both of these two fundamental human emotions. This is the simple and oh, so difficult choice. It is not an 'and' option, it can only be an 'or' option. Really simple, but...when our lower egoic selves get in the way of truly experiencing our life's purpose, we say, "Yes, but...." with the 'but' being the beginning of a negative thought or of a Fear choice. However, as one consciously recognizes and honours each act of LOVE, Fear loses its grip on our hearts, slipping away like taking off an old shoe that has hurt the foot for too long and needs to be replaced.

We all know, either consciously or subconsciously, that the only real reason why we chose to be here on Earth is to experience all the varieties and vagaries of LOVE. Why is it then so difficult for each one of us to consciously and intentionally always stay in the present moment and only choose to perceive all experiences as an opportunity for us to have more of what we came here to learn? Ah, this our challenge, our hero's journey – staying in the present moment – consciously paying attention to our intention – and choosing LOVE over FEAR. It really is quite simple when you think about it. We forget to think about why we are here and get caught up in the details of our lives often choosing from the Fear bucket feeling competition to be better than, bigger than, richer than, higher than, smarter than, and the list goes on.

This little missive is an example of how daily paying attention to one's intention and the little details that often go unnoticed can become one's main sustenance during the journey from one experience to another. I have chosen to pay attention to the little things. My friend, Dennis, once told me not to sweat the small stuff then he threw back his blonde-haired head and roared laughing, saying it was all small stuff. He was right. Our lives are only made up of small stuff. The big stuff we remember, the small stuff we overlook.

Well, this is an opportunity to identify your own 'small stuff' that makes a life while using the vignettes shared here as a jumping board for you to start your own collection of LOVE stories. When one focuses on the positive little events in one's life, it is amazing how these experiences pile up like the snowflakes and raindrops, and become very powerful reinforcements of what we are all about, what we are here to experience and to pay attention to, what we are here to learn.

You will have opportunity to write in this journal about your own LOVE experiences whether they be a feeling, a taste, a sight, a sound, a smell, a touch, or an intuition. Pay attention to your intention and you will find that choosing from the LOVE column is way more rewarding than even looking at the FEAR column. However, if you are not sure where an experience might fall, then the 80plus options per column are here for your benefit.

I hope that sharing my gifts of LOVE with you will activate you being more aware of when you receive such a gift of LOVE, too.

The following little vignettes are experiences of LOVE that I cherish. Many of these have happened after the Big event of my life -- since before that I was living in Fear and could not recognize these acts of LOVE. They may sound trivial. This is their power. Little things, subtly expressed with LOVE, create big results. Recognizing, honouring, and writing down the little acts of Love on a daily basis will help the reader to shift the perception from a position of doubt and fear to realize that most events have Love in them – the challenge is for each of us to take the time to recognize the gift and then to savour and honour it and take it into our hearts and lives.

January 1

"The best and most beautiful things in the world cannot be seen or even touched. They must be felt with the heart." Helen Keller

Lella G

I met Lella at a pot luck girl party. She came across as very bright, very particular, very engaging. Although not a literal person, she appeared to not suffer fools easily. Over time, I got to know a little bit about her life – however, only via the monthly girl parties. Over time, too, the people I originally met at the first girl party, changed, as anything does, and I did not see Lella at these parties. I did like her presence and missed it.

Having difficulty bending which made it extremely difficult to continue my own foot care, I called Lella, who I knew had a business called "Helping Hands," and asked if foot care was included. She immediately responded, "Yes!" The first time she came, she brought her own materials, soaked my feet, cut my toenails, filed them, rasped my heels of broken skin, massaged them with cream. I told her some of my life story. The second time she came, she used my materials, performed the same rituals and then put red polish on my nails. I asked her to tell me a story. She told me about her upbringing and her father's wonderful, if short, life in music, specifically performing organ music and teaching at the university. The third time she came, we again engaged in the foot ritual and exchanged more meaningful communications sharing snippets of each other's life stories back and forth. I had knit her a pair of leggings since she expressed interest in the ones I was knitting for myself a couple of months earlier. We talked about settling into one's living space and how books being available for access was so important to this feeling of settledness. She had not unpacked her books from a previous house renovation and was feeling it was time to do so.

All of this sharing of life story, caring contact of physical upkeep, the asking for help, the giving of help, and the receiving of help are pastels of images on the palette of Love.

****

Can you think of a similar event that you can choose to perceive as a gift of Love?

_____

_____

_____

_____

_____

_____

_____

_____

_____

_____

January 2

"Love, that most powerful and most popular of all the emotions, is both generated by the heart and received by the heart." Dr. Bradley Nelson

Richard G and Ian W

Sunday was the day, the day the beautiful blue spruce on my front lawn was coming down. In its prime, it had grown to be over 30 feet tall and with a shallow root system, was becoming unsafe in strong winds. Cradled in its upper limbs there were two crows' nests. My brother, Richard, had a portable chain saw and said he would come and cut it down. I did not know that he had never cut a tree this tall down before. I used to work with Ian and now that he, too, is retired, he helps me with yard work and odds and ends that need doing around the property. Richard's weakened wrists from a life-threatening motorcycle accident many years ago would have to do much of the controlling and pushing and pulling of the saw blade. Ian's father-in-law came and gave helpful suggestions to where to make the most appropriate cuts. Ian's wife, Nancy, came and held one of the rope lines on the tree while Ian guided the direction the tree would take after the cuts were done. The tree came down exactly where they had planned for it to come, then Richard de-limbed it. I then asked if he would chunk the length so that they would fit in my stove at no more than 15 inches. I knew this would tax his fragile wrists to the limit and hoped he knew he could certainly say 'no' not today. He started at the top end and as he came down the tree where it was getting wider and thicker, Ian put one of the already-cut pieces under the limb and then knelt and held the limb steady so Richard could cut through the harder pieces with more safety. Saw, chunk, lift, insert, hold, saw, chunk, lift, insert, hold, saw, and on it went. It took an hour and a half.

Afterward, I asked Richard how his wrists felt. He said they were vibrating and tingling. I could imagine that they would be aching badly as the day wore on. This act of helping is another colour of Love.

****

Can you think of a similar event that you can choose to perceive as a gift of Love?

_____

_____

_____

_____

_____

_____

_____

_____

_____

January 3

"For all of us, love can be the natural state of our own being; naturally at peace, naturally connected, because this becomes the reflection of who we simply are."
Sharon Salzberg

Chuck P

While facilitating an online college course, I was experiencing water in my basement. I whined this fact to an online adult student who immediately emailed back that he was sitting in his living room in his easy chair listening to his sump pump take the excess water from his basement outside. He then gave me the name and number of the person who had fixed his basement water seepage problems from the inside of the basement without destroying the outside landscaping around the house. I did get this one owner business to come and do the same process to my house so that I no longer have water in my basement. This student sharing this information was invaluable to me and my peace of mind. This is a hue of sharing Love.

****

Can you think of a similar event that you can choose to perceive as a gift of Love?

_____

_____

_____

_____

_____

_____

_____

_____

_____

_____

_____

_____

_____

_____

_____

January 4
"Teaching is a way to love others.   Learning is a way to love yourself."
Author Unknown

Gus A

After having a fireplace insert installed, getting wood to burn in it became a quest. Who to buy from? Who might be honourable with integrity? A friend gave me the name and telephone number of the person from whom she had been getting wood for a couple of years. I ordered my wood from him. When he brought the wood and put the truck dumper box up to allow gravity to force the wood to fall off, all went well until he started to drive the unit forward before putting the box down – which immediately got caught up in my clothesline and not only broke the clothesline but also shattered the 4x4 inch post that is part of the porch roof support as well. Being retired and on a fixed income and having come through some life-threatening health experiences, my reserves for stress were minimal. Gus came and looked at the damage and said when would be a good time for him to bring a carpenter friend to assess what needed to be done to fix it. My little self thought, "Yeah, right! When you drive out of here, I will never see or hear from you again." Oh, my little self is so skeptical and full of doubt. We made an appointment and sure enough Gus and his friend came and we three talked about options. We agreed on a plan and Gus told me to get the needed materials, including getting some heavy-duty iron 12-foot long railings made with holes in them to attach to the 4x4 inch wood support for the porch roof and he would reimburse me. Gus did absolutely everything he said he would do – everything. This is also what Love looks like, too.

****

Can you think of a similar event that you can choose to perceive as a gift of Love?

_____

_____

_____

_____

_____

_____

_____

_____

_____

_____

_____

_____

January 5
"Love doesn't sit there like a stone, it has to be made, like bread; remade all of the time, made new." Ursula K. LeGuin

Dr. David M

The third morning of my stay in the ICU where it still was not a sure thing that I would live, the admitting endocrinologist came in with the Head Nurse to check on me. After the obligatory question-and-answer-period, Dr. David looked at me with a smile on his face and asked if there was anything he could get me. What a question! What came to my mind instantly was a comfort from childhood – a popsicle, specifically an orange popsicle. He grinned and said, "I think we can arrange that." Within 10-15 minutes, the specialty nurse came with an orange popsicle. I haven't forgotten this tiny little extension of kindness, a form of Love, a way of hanging on to my life strings, attempting to keep me grounded on this Earth.

****

Can you think of a similar event that you can choose to perceive as a gift of Love?

_____

_____

_____

_____

_____

_____

_____

_____

_____

_____

_____

_____

_____

_____

_____

_____

January 6

"If we learn to open our hearts, anyone, including the people who drive us crazy, can be our teacher." Pema Chodron

Judy DeW

For at least two years, I attended classes and exercises and seminars and follow-ups at the Heart Function Clinic. The nurse running this program was and is, as they say, at the top of her game. She is caring, efficient, effective, cajoling, haranguing, cautious and ultimately very, very good at helping heart patients try to change life styles in order to prolong their time here on Earth. Whenever I went for a checkup with the specialist and there were blood results and heart test results, she always was very gracious in giving me physical copies of the results as I knew I would not remember them and could then review them later.

Her laugh made you want to join in the cadence. Her kindness made you feel special. This is another result of the power of Love.

****

Can you think of a similar event that you can choose to perceive as a gift of Love?

_____

_____

_____

_____

_____

_____

_____

_____

_____

_____

_____

_____

_____

_____

_____

_____

_____

January 7

"As you begin to understand the immense power and love you hold inside, you will find an unending surge of joy, light and love that will nourish and support you all the days of your life." Susan Jeffers

Leslie M

Jerusha invited me to join the monthly women's pot luck gatherings after I got some strength back from the near death encounter from untreated Graves' Disease and accompanying congestive heart failure. These gatherings are a wonderful sharing of energy and food and conversation. Two or three times a year, they are opened up for male energy to also be included. On one of these occasions, I met Leslie and her husband. Because Love has been such a large part of my healing process, in fact, the most important part, I tend to talk about what is most present in my life when asked. Leslie asked me what I did, the standard question, to which I replied that I was writing a book. She immediately shared the name of a friend of hers who had self-published and knew a lot about the process. Leslie generously sharing this information with me is also what Love sounds like, too.

****

Can you think of a similar event that you can choose to perceive as a gift of Love?

_____

_____

_____

_____

_____

_____

_____

_____

_____

_____

_____

_____

_____

_____

January 8
"The more I think about it, the more I realize there is nothing more artistic than to love others." Vincent van Gogh

Dennis and Toni C

After not dying, starting to get my breath back from being in Stage IV congestive heart failure, falling and breaking my left (dominant) wrist, all within a 10-month period, I thought a change of scenery would be a great idea. I took the train and went from Nova Scotia to Alberta stopping along the way, getting off and visiting friends and family for a couple of days and getting back on again to resume my trip. My destination was to visit Dennis and Toni in Alberta. They were the most gracious hosts, taking me to see their city of Edmonton, enjoying the company of interesting people while they allowed for my daily afternoon lie-downs to rest. On one occasion, they took me to the Old Strathcona Farmers' Market. This was an absolutely delightful experience where the venders made their booths look like paintings in how they arranged their wares for sale. They were always concerned about 'how I was doing', whether I needed more time to sight-see or to rest. They were the pent-ultimate tour hosts. Their care of me with my arm in a cast is what Love looks like, too.

****

Can you think of a similar event that you can choose to perceive as a gift of Love?

_____

_____

_____

_____

_____

_____

_____

_____

_____

_____

_____

_____

_____

January 9
"Where you find true friendship, you find true love." Author Unknown

Sheila F

Most of the time one can't seem to pinpoint where and when someone comes into one's life. Sheila came in to mine as a mature student looking to upgrade her skills. We hit it off and after we were no longer in a teacher-student situation, we became friends. When she graduated from the two-year community college program, she invited me to an outing on a little Cape Islander boat with 20 other people, none of whom I knew, to go across the rip tide from Scotman's Bay to Parrsboro. Being interested in photography, I thought this would be a great experience. The captain of the boat had one deck hand and we 20 passengers. There were no life jackets that I ever saw. The tide in the Bay of Fundy must have been at its peak of change, because as we went around Cape Split, the boat was almost swamped by roiling tide waters coming up over the boat from both of its sides as well as tide waters coming up over the boat from both its front and back. The little steering cabin became full with the captain and 21 other want-to-be-in-there, too, people trying to find relief from the cold salty waters washing over the boat as the captain had the engine at full throttle to keep us afloat. He was skilled. We were trusting. We made it out of the trough and across to Parrsboro and back with the outgoing tide. The experience was a thriller. This, too, is what Love feels like.

****

Can you think of a similar event that you can choose to perceive as a gift of Love?

_____

_____

_____

_____

_____

_____

_____

_____

_____

_____

_____

_____

_____

_____

January 10
"When you fall in love with someone else, you are falling in love with yourself, your essence that you see in someone else." Dr. Leon Masters

Marj H

You can live somewhere all your life and never feel part of the community – or you can be folded in like the ingredients of a cake batter. My neighbours, Marj and Philip, are the latter type. When I least expect it, the door bell will ring. I will go to see who is there. Marj will be standing at the door with a plate of some homemade treats in hand. She will come in, we will have tea, and we will have an old-fashioned visit where nothing of consequence is said or shared, yet everything about Love is conveyed – by manner, by gentleness, by laugh, by look, by the gift, by grace. These impromptu visits are another taste and look and feel of Love.

****

Can you think of a similar event that you can choose to perceive as a gift of Love?

_____

_____

_____

_____

_____

_____

_____

_____

_____

_____

_____

_____

_____

_____

_____

_____

_____

_____

January 11

"I feel that my mission is, wherever I am, to express my feeling about the importance of kindness, compassion, and the true sense of brotherhood. I practice these things. It gives me more happiness, more success. If I practiced anger or jealousy or bitterness, no doubt my smile would disappear." The Dalai Lama

Margaret and Bill W

The week after my accident and surgery to implant lots of metal and screws and bolts into my leg, my sister, Terry, who had moved in to look after me, wanted to take the evening off and visit her friend. My brother, Richard, offered to come and look after me. Just as the transition was being made and Terry drove out the driveway and Richard started coming into the bedroom to see what I might be wanting for supper, a knock came on the door. Richard went to see and came back to tell me he did not know who was there and should he let them in. I said yes. In came a small white-haired smiling woman and what was her tall smiling husband. Their names were Margaret and Bill and they were my neighbours across the busy highway whom I had yet to meet. She came right in through the porch, the kitchen and into my bedroom carrying a bowl of hot squash soup, warm recently-made bread buns, and warm up-side-down peach dumpling cake. It was Thanksgiving weekend and she had brought our supper as well and the next day's lunch. What a beautiful way in which to meet one's neighbours. Another gentle breeze of Love.

****

Can you think of a similar event that you can choose to perceive as a gift of Love?

January 12

"For true love is inexhaustible; the more you give, the more you have. And if you go to draw at the true fountainhead, the more water you draw, the more abundant is its flow."
Antoine de Saint-Exupery

Karen W

Sometimes love comes in unusual wrappings. Karen asked me to attend a rebuttal hearing with her as one of her silent witnesses while she attempted to make herself heard in a heart-wrenching saga between an insurance company and her employer. My challenge was that both the insurance company and her employer were former employers of mine. How do you not become attached to the hoped-for outcome that would allow your friend to be healed from a traumatic life event while at the same time, honouring previous relationships you have personally had. I had to let go and practice being in this world but not of it. To practice non-attachment. To honour my friend's journey with my presence while leaving any expectations for the outcome to the Universe to fulfill for my friend's highest good. Not an easy lesson to learn while physically present but mute while my friend's trauma is discounted and negated. She could not have known of my dilemma; however, in asking me to share her journey, if only briefly, she gave me a huge gift in another lesson about what Love looks like by allowing me to witness without engaging in her struggle.

****

Can you think of a similar event that you can choose to perceive as a gift of Love?

_____

_____

_____

_____

_____

_____

_____

_____

_____

_____

_____

_____

_____

_____

_____

January 13

"Some people never say the words 'I love you'. It's not their style to be so bold. Some people never say those words: 'I love you' but, like a child, they're longing to be told."
Paul Simon

Jamie and Jane G

As I lay in bed with my left leg in a cast from the surgery to implant the rod and 10 bolts and nuts to hold the shattered leg bones together while they healed, I thought about the work my brother and his wife had done in the last 24 hours of purchasing a bed rail, a portable commode, a walker, and a wheelchair and moving them all into my house, making my bedroom suitable for me to recuperate at home instead of being put in a nursing home as the attending surgeon suggested. This was so unbelievably comforting to be in my own home, in my own bed for this 6-month recuperation period of not being allowed to put any weight on my foot and leg. When I thought I was being moved 2 hours away from my family and my support systems for the 3-6 month period, I was devastated. Being shown Love by their actions was like being wrapped in a warmed blanket and coddled.

****

Can you think of a similar event that you can choose to perceive as a gift of Love?

_____

_____

_____

_____

_____

_____

_____

_____

_____

_____

_____

_____

_____

_____

January 14
"love builds up the broken wall
and straightens the crooked path.
love keeps the stars in the firmament
and imposes rhythm on the ocean tides
each of us is created of it
and i suspect
each of us was created for it"
Maya Angelou

Sheila F

When I was lying on the living room couch actively dying with my legs so swollen with fluid that the skin looked as if it might burst from the pressure, I asked Sheila to go to the drug store and buy a supply of elastic sports injury wraps. She did this. When she brought them in to the living room on her way home from work, I then asked her if she would tightly wrap my feet and legs up to the hips to try to get the fluid to move upwards. She is not a nurse. She is not a personal care worker. She is my friend. She took the elastoplasts and wrapped my feet and legs until I started to look like the bottom of a mummified body. It really didn't help with the fluid removal but it did take some of the pressure off the swollen skin and relieved some of the uncomfortableness. This is what Love looks and feels like, too.

****

Can you think of a similar event that you can choose to perceive as a gift of Love?

_____

_____

_____

_____

_____

_____

_____

_____

_____

_____

_____

_____

January 15
"A simple 'I love you' means more than money." Frank Sinatra

Mary R

During the first couple of weeks of my recovery, I had to learn how to get up out of bed with a leg cast on without bumping my leg, how to manoeuvre from the bed to a commode without putting any weight on my shattered leg, how to get in and out of a wheelchair, how to manoeuvre the wheelchair in and out of rooms that were never built to accommodate a wheelchair, how to reach the water taps in the kitchen sink, how to reach the wall electrical outlets over the kitchen counter, and on it went. A huge lesson in humility and resilience. Early on, my sister was my primary care-giver, a blessing I shall never forget. When there were times that she needed time off, I asked others to fill in, keeping me safe and accommodated. One such afternoon, Mary came to sit with me for a couple of hours. During that time, she was willing to take my removable cast off and to help me with my required exercises so my leg, ankle, and foot would not atrophy and seize up, to massage my leg and foot, and get my cast back into place. I could not do any of this for myself and her help was absolutely invaluable. A generosity of Love that helped me heal.

****

Can you think of a similar event that you can choose to perceive as a gift of Love?

_____

_____

_____

_____

_____

_____

_____

_____

_____

_____

_____

_____

_____

_____

January 16
"In doing something, do it with love or never do it at all." Mahatma Ghandi

Anne M

During the last valiant efforts of those who felt drawn to trying to save my life before the Universe stepped in and I chose to go to Emergency to see if intervention would help, several people came into my life who I had never met before – or who I might have heard of but not had contact with. Anne was one such person. My life-time friend's adult daughter went back to college and told me that I would like one of her instructors as she felt we had a lot of life orientation in common. When I was actively dying in Stage IV congestive heart failure, Anne appeared at my doorstep one day with a magnetic vest that she hoped might help my thyroid to calm down some and back off in its relentless effort to destroy my life. I felt so humble accepting this loaned gift and as I was so cold I immediately put the vest on. I wore it for many weeks although my health did not improve and, in fact, got worse, the intent of the gift of the vest was to help. Another cloak of Love.

****

Can you think of a similar event that you can choose to perceive as a gift of Love?

_____

_____

_____

_____

_____

_____

_____

_____

_____

_____

_____

_____

_____

_____

_____

_____

January 17
"It takes a lot to open up and love." Laura Bushnell

Richard G

When I woke up on the cement floor of a closed garage in February, holding my wrist and talking to myself saying "Go to your happy place," I knew that somehow I had to get myself to the hospital as this blackened, enlarged hand of mine needed help. Obviously, with help from somewhere else, I got myself up off the floor, got the garage door open by backing up to it with my rear end and pushing it open while walking backwards until I could get my good arm and hand up high enough to push it back on its rollers, got into the car and drove my standard-shift car to the hospital. There, I asked a nurse to phone my baby brother, Richard, to come to the hospital and stay with me. He did, no questions asked. We sat where they put us near the emergency entrance doors so that I was continually blasted with cold air whenever a new patient came in on a gurney with the sliding doors staying open long after they were into the hospital. He got them to bring me heated blankets to wrap around me. He would have gotten me water, anything to drink, if it had been allowed. It wasn't. We sat for 6 hours before my wrist was x-rayed, consultations made as to whether I needed pins put in via surgery or whether setting it and casting it would fix it, until finally after midnight, my wrist was pulled into position and a cast was put on it after I was given a miracle anesthetic that only took away any pain but not my awareness. Richard then drove me home and had his son, who he had called, drive my car back to my place. I was so thirsty and hungry that I insisted that he make me macaroni and cheese before they left. It was well after 1 a.m. by then. This is what Love looks like, too.

****

Can you think of a similar event that you can choose to perceive as a gift of Love?

_____

_____

_____

_____

_____

_____

_____

_____

_____

_____

_____

January 18
"I never knew how to worship until I knew how to love." Henry Ward Beecher

Lorna N

The saying is that people come in to your life for a reason. Lorna was a participant in a love course that I happened to be invited to join. One day she had a bad shoulder, perhaps from working with the horses too vigorously. At this time in my life, I was learning about how to use 'love energy' to heal. I had serendipitously been following a Qi Gong healer on a webinar and had learned how to direct loving thoughts through my fingers toward a challenged physical part. Lorna allowed me to practice this directing of healing energy, known as sword fingers, to her hurting shoulder. She could not know what a gift of love she was giving me in trusting that I had the knowledge, skill, and ability to attempt to help while doing no harm in the process. This act of Love helped my self-confidence and strengthened my resolve to learn as many ways to help myself and others as possible.

****

Can you think of a similar event that you can choose to perceive as a gift of Love?

_____

_____

_____

_____

_____

_____

_____

_____

_____

_____

_____

_____

_____

_____

_____

_____

January 19

"If you add a little to a little, and then do it again, soon that little shall be much."
Hesiod

Dr. Ed H

When I tried to stop my car from rolling down a raggedy gravely sloped incline by running around the car, yanking the driver's door open, and attempting to leap into the car to put my right foot on the brake, my left leg went out from under me at a right angle to the knee joint while my right leg slid under the car. Knowing that my left leg was hurt and that if I let go of the car my right leg would be also hurt by the car running over it, I hung on and went with the car – down the hill. When I arrived at the hospital, I was gifted with the most capable and gentle-spoken orthopedic surgeon. I was not in good shape, having just survived Stage IV congestive heart failure a year previously. The surgeon could not find an anesthesiologist who was willing to put me under for the reconstructive surgery for almost three days. During these days I lay on a stretcher in the hallway with no food, no liquids, no treatment. When three nurses had tried seven times to put an IV drip in my arm on the second day and failed, Dr. Ed came along, took the butterfly needle and with one jab, successfully inserted a line to allow saline liquid into my body. His skill and dexterity performed with compassion are also what Love feels like.

****

Can you think of a similar event that you can choose to perceive as a gift of Love?

January 20

"Just because somebody doesn't love you the way you want them to, doesn't mean they don't love you with all they have." Author Unknown

Linda B

At one point in my writing career, I needed to have US stamps to include in a package to a prospective publisher so I could have the manuscript returned to me. One cannot just go to any Canadian postal outlet and buy US stamps that can be mailed in the United States. No. This is not possible. Linda, my friend in Dallas, Texas, obliged me by sending me the appropriate US stamps for me to include in my package. She probably views this little act of kindness as "nothing;" however, for me not being able to get the stamps any other way short of driving nine hours to go over the Canadian/US border to purchase them, she helped me out immensely. I look on this as another expression of Love.

****

Can you think of a similar event that you can choose to perceive as a gift of Love?

_____

_____

_____

_____

_____

_____

_____

_____

_____

_____

_____

_____

_____

_____

January 21
"Passion makes the world go round. Love just makes it a safer place." Ice T

VON lady

The local Victoria Order of Nurses' organization at first sent a nurse every day for the first week and then would send a nurse every other day to take the cast and the bandage off the 108 staples down the front of my leg's incision, clean it and replace the bandage and put the cast back on. One such nurse (there were several of them and it was hard to remember their names – although I will always remember their gentleness and effectiveness) told me about a product that would help the twelve-inch scar fade that could be gotten over the counter of a local department store. I would never have known about this opportunity – never. This sharing is what Love looks like.

****

Can you think of a similar event that you can choose to perceive as a gift of Love?

_____

_____

_____

_____

_____

_____

_____

_____

_____

_____

_____

_____

_____

_____

_____

_____

_____

January 22

"Love is the master key that opens the gates of happiness." Oliver Wendell Holmes

Jane G

The first weekend after I was moved home with my shattered leg in a cast and my sister moved in to look after me, my brother, Jamie, and my sister-in-law, Jane, telephoned to ask if we would like them to bring supper. Of course, we said yes. They brought fish and chips from a restaurant I had not eaten at before. They brought everything: plates of food, bowls of coleslaw, napkins, utensils – and their caring smiles. I was put in the wheelchair and wheeled into the living room where we sat and ate our shared meal. My heart opened more that day with this unfolding of Love.

****

Can you think of a similar event that you can choose to perceive as a gift of Love?

_____

_____

_____

_____

_____

_____

_____

_____

_____

_____

_____

_____

_____

_____

_____

_____

_____

January 23
"Love is patient and kind; love is not jealous or boastful; it is not arrogant or rude.
[I Corinthians]" Bible

Donna R

Donna and I had shared residence rooms when doing our teachers' certification while adults. We had travelled together. We had taught the same subjects and shared materials and aids to teaching. We had shared drives together, shared personal stories together.

When I came home from the hospital, still alive, from the untreated Graves' Disease-induced congestive heart failure, I was very, very weak. Since my heart was not functioning at all well and I was on many heavy-duty drugs, one thing became clear.

Since I didn't die when all the indications were that I would and should have, then, while I was still here, I needed to figure out how to be as well as I could be so that I could have quality of life at this stage of my life journey.

Donna, being a now former colleague, phoned to see if I was at home and said she was coming to visit. When she came, she brought with her a large cooler full of food – not just any food – we are talking top of the line food – salmon steaks, vegetables, grains, meats, eggs, what all was in that cooler was also augmented by another large bag of a collection of foodstuffs. I was and still am dumbfounded. I have never seen such a large amount of foodstuffs pour out of a cooler like these did. She unloaded all of these nutritious gifts and then quickly left. I have never been able to repay her gifts and can only write about them here as they were more examples of what Love looks, smells, and tastes like.

****

Can you think of a similar event that you can choose to perceive as a gift of Love?

_____

_____

_____

_____

_____

_____

_____

_____

_____

_____

_____

_____

January 24
"Love one another and you will be happy. It's as simple and as difficult as that."
Michael Leunig

Brenda D

How do people come into your life? This one time I do remember when and how Brenda came into my life. I had stopped at a local farmer's market to get some Dragon's Breath cheese about which I had heard. As I was looking around, Brenda came in. Since we knew other people in common, we said hi. She asked how I was and I started in on what had happened to me in the last year since I retired and how I was doing now and that I had heard about an exciting exercise routine called QiGong and I had started doing the gently stretching and balancing exercises. She said she would be interested in trying it and could she come by one night after her work. Of course, I thought this would be great to have someone to help motivate me and to share in the experience and make it more meaningful. I did not know this Brenda and wondered if she kept her word or if I might not hear or see from her, but, she called the next week and came over late one afternoon to try QiGong with me. Well! She came once, twice, three times a week and has even come four and five times a week. What a gift! My motivation is not that strong without some external stimulus. Brenda coming, sitting and having a glass of warm water and sharing life happenings, then doing the QiGong exercise routine is a beautiful reinforcement of the power of Love.

****

Can you think of a similar event that you can choose to perceive as a gift of Love?

_____

_____

_____

_____

_____

_____

_____

_____

_____

_____

_____

_____

January 25

"There is always something left to love. And if you haven't learned that, you ain't learned nothing." Lorraine Hansberry

Rene K

As 6 months went by after the big event and my survival, my former next door neighbour called and invited me for lunch on the Sunday. I arrived to the most wondrous meal. Creamed peas on toast with white sauce. Not just any creamed peas but seriously created and beautifully tasting creamed peas with egg, and, and, and. We sat with lace tablecloth, cloth napkins, crystal glasses, china dinnerware and ate creamed peas on toast along with juice and coffee. I could not remember ever having this dish and the comfort it brought on of being safe was astonishing. A bread basket of Love.

****

Can you think of a similar event that you can choose to perceive as a gift of Love?

_____

_____

_____

_____

_____

_____

_____

_____

_____

_____

_____

_____

_____

_____

January 26
"I get the best feeling in the world when you say hi or even smile at me because I know, even if it's just for a second, that I've crossed your mind." Author Unknown

Jon C

I knew Karen long before I met Jon. Jon and Karen met and married when they were in their forties. It took awhile for me to learn about Jon and for Jon to learn about me. We have now known each other for 30 years or more. He has had some major health challenges and I, too, have had some major physical learning opportunities. What Jon can and does do is keep in touch by email, even though he and Karen only live a little less than one hour from me. Whenever I open my emails and see one from Jon, I know it will bring a smile to my face and probably a laugh-out-loud sound from my throat. You see, Jon shares really, really good funny jokes with me. It could be a TV advertisement that is running in Europe, or it could be a spoof he found on YouTube: it could be anything he finds funny that he knows would tickle my quirky sense of humour – so, he shares and sends it along which often makes my day. He doesn't know it, but, I do. These are acts of Love that I treasure greatly.

****

Can you think of a similar event that you can choose to perceive as a gift of Love?

_____

_____

_____

_____

_____

_____

_____

_____

_____

_____

_____

_____

January 27
"He that plants trees loves others besides himself." English Proverb

Theresa S

I had the same tenants for more than nine years sharing my house space by living upstairs with their two kitty cats, Tigger and Diamond first, then Tigger and Lanny. After the leg accident and I was in a wheelchair for 6 months which coincided with the Fall and Winter seasons, I was unable to push the large waste management food recyclable green cart out to the roadside every two weeks for collection. My tenant, Theresa, offered to do this since it benefited the both of us. After my leg healed enough to resume many of my routine activities, Theresa continued to not only push the green cart out to roadside, but also came around the back of the house to check if I had any recyclable bags and/or garbage bags outside to go out to the roadside and if I had anything sitting at the top of the steps, she would come and get them and take them out, too. We never really talked about this little act of love, but I will always remember how such a seemingly small act of kindness makes my heart feel full with Love.

****

Can you think of a similar event that you can choose to perceive as a gift of Love?

_____

_____

_____

_____

_____

_____

_____

_____

_____

_____

_____

_____

_____

_____

January 28
"The weak can never forgive. Forgiveness is the attribute of the strong." Gandhi

Eliz C

Learning how to be a compassionate office manager was a whole lot harder than learning how to do a multimillion dollar budget. Being brought up to never ask for help and to give the appearance of innately knowing how to do something perfectly the first time it is tried, puts a huge burden on one's psyche, as well as setting up one for huge opportunities to pile on the guilt and shame. I had been an office manager for close to six years when one of my assistants took me aside and told me most of the staff who reported to me were afraid of me. I was absolutely shocked and devastated. My fragile self-image took an almost mortal blow. To this day over 40 years later, I still remember how kind and gentle Eliz was in sharing this feedback with me. It was an act of courage on her part to which I have always been eternally grateful. What I heard was such a strong affirmation that I was worth knowing this information so that I could incorporate change in to my daily life for all our sakes. What a supreme act of Love.

****

Can you think of a similar event that you can choose to perceive as a gift of Love?

_____

_____

_____

_____

_____

_____

_____

_____

_____

_____

_____

_____

_____

January 29

"Every time you smile at someone, it is an action of love, a gift to that person, a beautiful thing." Mother Theresa

Dr. Russell and Heidi G

Every one has a song in his/her heart and every song should be sung out loud. That some people's songs do not sound the same as other people's songs is no reason for them not to sing. My brother, Russell, has such a unique heart song voice. On my 65th birthday, he and his wife, Heidi, telephoned me from away and sang. They sang Happy Birthday to me over the telephone. It was a cascading waterfall of sound rippling over my heart. This, too, is what Love looks, or should I say – sounds? like.

****

Can you think of a similar event that you can choose to perceive as a gift of Love?

_____

_____

_____

_____

_____

_____

_____

_____

_____

_____

_____

_____

_____

_____

January 30
"Love is the poetry of the senses." Honore de Balzac

Jamie G

At one point my house boy suggested a former colleague of his from whom I could get cut wood for the winter. I called. The person came and insisted on being paid before delivery. I felt that I should not do this – but I did. Another lesson in the making. He never did deliver, but took my money. I was whining to my mother about this one day and she suggested I ask Jamie. if he had any suggestions of what I might do to rectify this – short of going to court. About a week after talking with Jamie a truck came into my driveway, backing up to the edge, and then a man got out and started having the truck's back container lift up to release cut wood onto the ground. I went out to ask him who he was and if he was at a wrong address. He said no, this was from Jamie and gave me a copy of an invoice that he said was already paid. I was so taken with this visible act of Love that I wrote the following poem:

My eyes cry   i, I, eye, oh, Jamie
My breath catches   Gentle maker
My mind whys   Of it better.
My heart sighs
I'm so surprised.

My eyes cry
My breath catches
My mind sighs
My heart blesses
Maker of fire.

****

Can you think of a similar event that you can choose to perceive as a gift of Love?

_____

_____

_____

_____

_____

_____

_____

_____

_____

_____

January 31
"The best proof of love is trust." Dr. Brothers

Daddy G

I was upstairs in Mom and Dad's room where I had picked up Dad's Gibson guitar. I was trying to make my fingers stretch the distances to wrap my hand around the neck in order to pick out a tune. It seemed to be very difficult. I could pick easier than try to play a chord. Dad heard the 'noise' from downstairs and came upstairs where he asked me what I was doing. I said I was trying to pick out a tune on his guitar. He said, "Well, if you are going to try to play, you need the guitar restrung since you are left-handed and the guitar is strung for me, right-handed." He did restring the guitar so that I could try to play. It was so much easier that way! The sound of Love.

****

Can you think of a similar event that you can choose to perceive as a gift of Love?

_____

_____

_____

_____

_____

_____

_____

_____

_____

_____

_____

_____

_____

_____

_____

_____

_____

February 1
"Love is like a virus. It can happen to anybody at any time." Maya Angelou

Jamie G

With the lovely back lawn only producing grass to be mowed, I thought it would be nice to have some vegetables growing for my use. Because I was still compromised from the leg shattering experience, I asked Jamie if he would come prepare a 10-foot long, 4-foot wide swatch so I could grow cucumbers and tomatoes. He not only came and hand dug up the space, turning the sod over, then putting farm manure he had brought from his own animals in the mix, then smoothing it all down, he also put up a lovely trellis-type of netting for the cucumbers to grow up so that I would not have to harvest them from the ground. Then, he planted. I have pictures of him with his spade digging up the ground and making the garden space ready for planting. This is what Love looks like, too – and that summer after harvest, this was also was Love tasted like when I harvested his gifts.

****

Can you think of a similar event that you can choose to perceive as a gift of Love?

_____

_____

_____

_____

_____

_____

_____

_____

_____

_____

_____

_____

_____

_____

_____

February 2

"The more anger towards the past you carry in your heart, the less capable you are of loving in the present." Barbara de Angelis

Lora S

In the 1980s I consulted with American Airlines in Oklahoma over a two-year time frame. The supervisor I worked with disliked me on sight as I was hired to help her 'do her job better'. It took some time for us to come to a mutual understanding of our roles and that we could, in fact, assist one another. After that, there was no turning back. We became friends. Many times that I worked there, it would be over a two or three-week time frame which meant I was there over the weekend(s). One weekend, Lora suggested she take me on a drive to the Arkansas corner of Oklahoma to get a sense of the State where she had lived as a child. We spent the whole day together, driving, stopping and looking, talking, experiencing, eating until we arrived at a place where there were some rocks. Oklahoma, where she lived, did not have any rocks, only sandy gravel. We managed to get one medium-sized boulder in to the trunk of the car to bring back for her property as a reminder of her home State. It has now been more than 30 years since that day's drive; however, I still remember the feelings and sights and the weight of that rock we lifted in to her car. This, too, is what Love feels and looks like.

****

Can you think of a similar event that you can choose to perceive as a gift of Love?

_____

_____

_____

_____

_____

_____

_____

_____

_____

_____

_____

_____

_____

February 3
"A true friend never gets in your way unless you happen to be going down."
Arnold H. Glasgow

Debbie P

My Queen of Clean who actually found rubber gloves with this phrase on the wrist bands, came in to my life via her sister. When I was wondering how to cut down on the drafts that waft through my older house, she said she would bring something the next time she came that would help. I thought no more of this statement until two weeks later when she arrived with a bag of little white, what looked like, plugs for electrical outlets. Now, I am the daughter of an electrician; however, I had not known of these draft-saving devices. She brought enough to plug every receptacle that did not have a plug in it throughout my whole house. This, too, is what Love feels like when the drafts are closed off.

****

Can you think of a similar event that you can choose to perceive as a gift of Love?

_____

_____

_____

_____

_____

_____

_____

_____

_____

_____

_____

_____

_____

_____

_____

_____

February 4
"There can be no deep disappointment where there is not deep love."
Martin Luther King

Ella F

As I regained my strength and mobility, I had two cords of wood delivered to the driveway where it sat all spring and summer. It was now September. My life-time friend who baby-sat her youngest grand-child and was at the house when he went on the bus in the morning and was sure to be at the house when he arrived back home on the bus in the early afternoon, offered to take the bus and come down and help me put some of the wood in the basement. We put 20 sticks of wood in the wheelbarrow, wheeled it across the driveway to the cellar way entrance of 6 steps, dumped it into the entrance, went back and got another 20 sticks of wood until we had 100 sticks of wood piled up on the basement steps. Then we went down to the basement and carried the wood over to the other side of the cellar and stacked them. We did this until we were too tired to handle the wheelbarrow without dumping the wood any where but in the cellar way entrance. Another colour of Love.

****

Can you think of a similar event that you can choose to perceive as a gift of Love?

_____

_____

_____

_____

_____

_____

_____

_____

_____

_____

_____

_____

_____

_____

_____

February 5
"A heart that loves is always young." Greek Proverb

Dr. Russell G

When I was actively dying at a pretty quick pace, I was at my parents' place to celebrate my father's birthday and my own since they are two days apart. After a lovely meal, my brother 'from away' started telling me that I was really ill and needed to go to the emergency room of the local hospital. He was forceful in his voice when saying this. He said that he felt if I didn't agree, he and others in the family should physically take me and have me treated even if it was against my will. This so incensed me that my own desires and wishes were not being honoured that I lashed back at him in words and voice. I was brutal. We were playing kitchen bridge at the time and I got up from the table and left the house. He was still shouting that he wanted to take me to the hospital to save my life as I drove away. At the time, I felt he was imposing his desire to control on my desire to die. Now, I realize that he was trying to say he loved me and wanted me to live. I thank him for his honesty of heart. This, too, is what Love sounds like.

****

Can you think of a similar event that you can choose to perceive as a gift of Love?

February 6
"Love is a fabric which never fades, no matter how often it is washed in the water of adversity and grief." Author Unknown

Lella G

When I originally thought that perhaps I didn't die so I could share my stories with others, I started a little story about love from which I needed some feedback. I mentioned this need to Lella on one of our encounters. She immediately put me in touch with her friend, Anne, a lovely, astute writer who also happens to teach at the local university. Not only was Anne willing to read my first attempt, she came to my house and gave me very insightful feedback that helped me to realize my orientation needed to be reworked. She was very gentle in her discussion for which I am truly grateful. Lella knew exactly what I needed and had the connection and trust of her friend who she offered without reservation. This, too, is what Love looks like.

****

Can you think of a similar event that you can choose to perceive as a gift of Love?

_____

_____

_____

_____

_____

_____

_____

_____

_____

_____

_____

_____

_____

_____

_____

_____

February 7
"Perhaps they are not stars, but rather openings in heaven where the love of our lost ones pours through and shines down upon us to let us know they are happy."
Eskimo Proverb

Simon

I am guessing that the neighbourhood news trickled into the local Post Office that my original accident, where I shattered my leg, happened while getting my mail from the new local super box for mail delivery. After this, whenever there was more mail than my little mail box would hold or there was a piece of mail that had to be signed for, instead of receiving a notice in the mail to go to the local Post Office to get my mail, a tall English blonde-haired man named Simon would arrive at my door with personal delivery. This has continued to happen long after my leg has healed. What colour of Love might this be? Green? for the heart chakra? Probably.

****

Can you think of a similar event that you can choose to perceive as a gift of Love?

_____

_____

_____

_____

_____

_____

_____

_____

_____

_____

_____

_____

_____

_____

_____

_____

February 8

"This is the miracle that happens every time to those who really love; the more they give, the more they possess." Rainer Maria Rilke

Susun W

I am told time and time again the Universe only gives you what you really need when you are ready to really receive. This was the way with a natural helper in the form of a wild plant that started growing outside my house door right after I was diagnosed with high-risk osteoporosis. It had never been here for the previous 12 years I have lived here. It only came after I found I could not take calcium supplements as they caused problems with my heart.

In order to identify the plant I went online and found Susun on YouTube. She described the plant and called it stinging nettle and explained its healing properties, especially as they relate to calcium, other minerals, and strong bones. She also gave a demonstration of how to harvest and use the plant's leaves to make a tea infusion. All this was a totally new experience for me. I did all she suggested, continue to do so, including harvesting and freezing to continue making the tea infusions throughout the winter months, too. This is what Love looks and tastes like.

****

Can you think of a similar event that you can choose to perceive as a gift of Love?

February 9
"Do you wish to be anything except what you are." St. Francis

Terry Z

John and I had been talking for over an hour on the telephone while it was cold and dreary outside and the fire in the fireplace warmed the living room. At some point, I felt a presence in the room with me. I looked to the door and there stood Terry, holding out a gift. She had driven almost 2 hours and had dropped in to my place without me knowing she was coming to share her copy of a bridge game. What a gift! We visited and then she left to get home before it got dark. I love her. Another expression of Love.

****

Can you think of a similar event that you can choose to perceive as a gift of Love?

_____

_____

_____

_____

_____

_____

_____

_____

_____

_____

_____

_____

_____

_____

_____

_____

_____

_____

February 10

"Love is what we are born with. Fear is what we learn. The spiritual journey is the unlearning of fear and prejudices and the acceptance of love back in our hearts. Love is the essential reality and our purpose on earth. To be consciously aware of it, to experience love in ourselves and others, is the meaning of life. Meaning does not lie in things. Meaning lies in us." Marianne Williamson

Rene K

When I asked Rene to become a fourth to play bridge, I did not know that she had never played. She said yes she would come and has been absolutely amazing in the first two games we have played, learning super quickly, making great plays, asking astute questions. She says she is wandering around in the dark not knowing what she is doing or what to do. I say she is doing great and that this is another form of Love to try something you know absolutely nothing about just because someone asked you to, and to continue with it, sharing of her presence while in a very steep learning curve. Wonderful to see her vulnerable and going for it anyway.

****

Can you think of a similar event that you can choose to perceive as a gift of Love?

February 11
"If it is true that there are as many minds as there are heads, then there are as many kinds of love as there are hearts." Leo Tolstoy

Binnie and Wanda L

I think the Universe makes it a point to help those who are too afraid to see love around them by breaking their shells open so that the light can come in. When I was attempting to stay alive after the heroic resuscitation at the local hospital to counteract my near death experience, people came to show their love in so many ways that I am still so utterly amazed – and so grateful – at the number of people and the variety of ways they chose.

Binnie and Wanda were acquaintances yet they came to the hospital, left a plush Tigger toy for me to cuddle in the bed, then after I came home, they came again many times, bringing home-made foodstuffs, a prayer pillow, and another stuffed Lion toy for me. I don't remember having plush toys as a child and in my newly-recreated existence, these stuffed animals are very precious to me. They, too, feel like Love.

****

Can you think of a similar event that you can choose to perceive as a gift of Love?

_____

_____

_____

_____

_____

_____

_____

_____

_____

_____

_____

_____

_____

_____

February 12

"Love alone is capable of uniting living beings in such a way as to complete and fulfill them, for it alone takes them and joins them by what is deepest in themselves."
Pierre Teilhard de Chardin

Doug G

After the shattered leg got well enough so that I could bend again and feed the airtight fireplace insert stove, I went back to heating my space my wood-burning instead of using oil-fired heat. The first year was a steep learning curve and I didn't have enough wood to last the winter season so I was buying and burning weather-wet and sap-wet wood. This type of wood does not burn well and does not give good heat.

A friend's husband was doing some renovations in their basement and they had left-over lumber that Doug cut up and brought in boxes to my house throughout that winter to help with the wet wood burning. This is what Love feels like – warm, embracing heat.

****

Can you think of a similar event that you can choose to perceive as a gift of Love?

_____

_____

_____

_____

_____

_____

_____

_____

_____

_____

_____

_____

_____

_____

_____

_____

February 13
"Love the giver more than the gift." Brigham Young

Jerusha Y

Jerusha practices massage therapy using an osteopathic approach. I am gifted with her treatments on a regular basis. One of these times when we were finished the session, she asked if I had worn socks. I answered that I had. She then got them and lovingly put them on my feet, knowing how difficult it is for me to bend my back and hips and knees and ankles to do this simple act of dressing. This is what Love feels like, too.

****

Can you think of a similar event that you can choose to perceive as a gift of Love?

_____

_____

_____

_____

_____

_____

_____

_____

_____

_____

_____

_____

_____

_____

_____

_____

_____

February 14

"Your task is not to seek for love, but merely to seek and find all the barriers within yourself that you have built against it." Jalal Rumi

Jane G

When another gift from the Universe came my way in the form of a medical doctor who practices biological medicine, one of the suggestions made to help my body recover from years of abuse was to sit in an infared sauna to help detox through sweat coming out the pores of my skin. In general conversation, I mentioned this to Jane, having no idea that she and her husband actually had such a sauna that they used regularly for just such purposes. She offered that I could come and use their sauna for my own healing. Another expression of Love in the feel of healing heat.

****

Can you think of a similar event that you can choose to perceive as a gift of Love?

_____

_____

_____

_____

_____

_____

_____

_____

_____

_____

_____

_____

_____

_____

_____

_____

_____

February 15
"By this all men will know that you are my disciples, if you have love for one another.
[John 13:35]" Bible

Anne M

I was so honoured to be asked to join a little group for a couple of months around the full moon to share in a meditation accompanied by Anne playing her crystal bowls. If one were to think of what it might sound like in Heaven, then the sounds of the crystal bowls would be one of those sounds. I am so thankful that Anne asked me to experience this sound of Love.

****

Can you think of a similar event that you can choose to perceive as a gift of Love?

_____

_____

_____

_____

_____

_____

_____

_____

_____

_____

_____

_____

_____

_____

_____

_____

_____

_____

February 16
"In real love you want the other person's good. In romantic love you want the other person." Margaret Anderson

Gordie W

On a visit to see my husband's great-uncle, Gordie, I noticed a really beautiful black sculpture of this African native in a crouch position with a spear in his hand. I mentioned how beautiful I thought it was. Gordie insisted that I take this sculpture with me when we left. I still have this beautiful reminder of his expression of Love.

****

Can you think of a similar event that you can choose to perceive as a gift of Love?

_____

_____

_____

_____

_____

_____

_____

_____

_____

_____

_____

_____

_____

_____

_____

_____

_____

_____

February 17

"Love means to commit oneself without guarantee, to give oneself completely in the hope that our love will produce love in the loved person. Love is an act of faith, and whoever is of little faith is also of little love." Erich Fromm

Leslen S

You know those times when you are around someone for a long period of time and yet you do not know the person? Leslen and I were part of a group of over 40 people who spent 6-9 weeks together touring Europe in a bus. It was not until the last night in Amsterdam, Holland, that Leslen and I finally connected and, boy, did we connect. We stayed up all night talking. Since then I have visited her in Missouri and she has visited me here in Nova Scotia. Our European student bus tour was in 1978. We have known each other for more than 35 years. Every year, I get a Christmas card from her that is a picture of her and her family, husband, children, and maybe this year – grandchildren. This is what Love looks like, too.

****

Can you think of a similar event that you can choose to perceive as a gift of Love?

_____

_____

_____

_____

_____

_____

_____

_____

_____

_____

_____

_____

_____

_____

_____

_____

February 18

"For beautiful eyes, look for the good in others; for beautiful lips, speak only words of kindness; and for poise, walk with the knowledge that you are never alone."
Audrey Hepburn

Fran O

I met Fran on an European bus tour. One of the stipulations in order to be considered for the tour group was that one was studying something. Fran was 50 years old at the time and a principal of an elementary school in California. She was also working on a Masters Degree and this tour entitled anyone taking it to pick up an art and history credit. Even though I was not close to her age as some others, she and I became friends. I have been to visit her in California and she has been to visit me here in Nova Scotia. We have enjoyed chatty letters over the years and cards filled up with all the white space used to exchange our lives' journeys. Even though I do not see Fran, I still think of the fun things we did and the memories we shared together from drinking new wine in a grotto in Austria to swimming in the Aegean Sea off Greece. I treasure these experiences shared with Fran and this, too, is what Love feels like.

****

Can you think of a similar event that you can choose to perceive as a gift of Love?

_____

_____

_____

_____

_____

_____

_____

_____

_____

_____

_____

_____

_____

_____

February 19
"Hate the sin and love the sinner." Mahatma Ghandi

Breanna M

Having never been a grandmother to my genetic grandchildren, I was telling this to the mother of Breanna. Melissa, Breanna's mother, said she would ask her daughter if she would like to have another grandmother for her to-be-born first child. She said 'yes'. That child, Jacob, is now with us, and his smell and smile are what Love look like, too. Thank you to Breanna for saying 'yes'.

****

Can you think of a similar event that you can choose to perceive as a gift of Love?

_____

_____

_____

_____

_____

_____

_____

_____

_____

_____

_____

_____

_____

_____

_____

_____

_____

_____

_____

February 20
"Fail at love, and the other tests don't matter." Richard Bach

Tim T

When I moved from renting a duplex to buying a house, there were many things at the new-to-me house that needed attention. Tim and his wife had taken over the renting of the duplex where I had been, and had bought a couple of things that I wanted to leave there. When I found out that Tim was a Mr. Fix-it, I asked him if he might help me install some patio stones as a walkway from the driveway to the front steps and main entrance. He not only helped me, he did the work, beautifully. And, then he went on to help me with several other projects that needed attention such as the water leak that was showing up on a main floor room ceiling. He realized this was from a seepage of water around the upstairs window sash, hung out the window, and caulked this problem into a solution. He came in to my life at the exact time that I needed someone with his particular skills and he helped me. This, too, is what Love looks like.
****

Can you think of a similar event that you can choose to perceive as a gift of Love?

_____

_____

_____

_____

_____

_____

_____

_____

_____

_____

_____

_____

_____

_____

_____

_____

February 21

"The day the child realizes that all adults are imperfect, he becomes an adolescent; the day he forgives them, he becomes an adult; the day he forgives himself, he becomes wise." Alden Nowlan

Errol Z

For many years, the same elderly man has brought his ¾ ton truck with the snowplow on the front and ploughed my driveway. After my congestive heart failure episode, he started wanting to shovel off my 10 steps into the house. I gave him a shovel. From there on after, every time he came to plough, he got out of the truck afterward and shoveled off my 10 steps, then went over in front of the garage where the car was stored, and shoveled the door to it accessible and then went over to the shed where the generator was stored and hand-shoveled this access, too. He is not a young or healthy man, yet he assiduously did these loving actions on my behalf. I treasure him for these actions of Love.

****

Can you think of a similar event that you can choose to perceive as a gift of Love?

_____

_____

_____

_____

_____

_____

_____

_____

_____

_____

_____

_____

_____

_____

February 22
"Familiar acts are beautiful through love." Percy Bysshe Shelley

Andy D

After I didn't die from Stage IV congestive heart failure, the local Heart Function Clinic suggested that I might benefit from joining the 10-week program including exercises, nutrition, drug discussions, and general association with others in similar circumstances. There is always strength in groups.

Andy was one of the patients doing the 10-week program. Spouses would occasionally also attend sessions. We met twice a week. Andy was one of the people who encouraged me when I had no breath or strength to continue on many of those occasions.

Afterward, Andy took up nature photography with a passion and I went on some of his walks to look for items to photograph. He had a natural affinity to photographing birds and kept a yearly bird count that numbered in the hundreds. From his first foray, he sent an email of where, when, and what he had done on a particular walk with attachments of his photography. His photography is exquisite and ever so beautiful. This is definitely what Love looks like.

****

Can you think of a similar event that you can choose to perceive as a gift of Love?

_____

_____

_____

_____

_____

_____

_____

_____

_____

_____

_____

_____

_____

_____

February 23
"The spaces between your fingers were created so that another's could fill them in."
Author Unknown

Bob H

Bob and I shared a cubicle partition while working. He exuded gentleness and a very dry wit. He also exhibits just plain old kindness. One of these surprise kindnesses was a telephone call to tell me one of our colleagues was retiring and would I like him to pick me up and take me to the retirement luncheon. Of course, I said, Yes, please, and so he did. After the luncheon, he drove me around the area showing me where he used to live many years ago and telling me little snippets about his life then. He finally brought me home and I had had a wonderful outing and lovely afternoon touring the country roads with a very kind and gentle caretaker. This is what Love feels like, too.

****

Can you think of a similar event that you can choose to perceive as a gift of Love?

_____

_____

_____

_____

_____

_____

_____

_____

_____

_____

_____

_____

_____

February 24
"Paradise is always where love dwells." Jean Richter

Peter M

Toward the end of my tenure teaching at the local community college, I was working late one Friday night at the beginning of a long weekend. The air conditioning had been turned off for the weekend and since it was September, I found it extremely stifling in my little cubicle. The fact that I was having a hyperthyroidism crisis probably also contributed to this heat exhaustion. When I was walking down the corridor to leave the building, I felt weak and started to faint. The Universe is so accommodating in giving what we need and only when we need it. Peter was coming along on his way out for the long weekend just at this time. He caught me as I fell. This, too, is what Love does.

****

Can you think of a similar event that you can choose to perceive as a gift of Love?

_____

_____

_____

_____

_____

_____

_____

_____

_____

_____

_____

_____

_____

_____

_____

_____

February 25

"One who does what the friend wants done will never need a friend." Rumi

Marj H

As I sit here doing the work of my life writing this book, saying to myself, you need to get up, you have been sitting for more than 5 hours, you need to get something to drink, your mouth is dry, the bell at the door rings. I get up and there is my next door neighbour with warm, just made, tea biscuits, and a hug. How did she know? We caught up on her husband's condition in hospital, said we loved each other, hugged, and parted. This is what Love smells like, feels like, sounds like, looks like, and now, tastes like.

****

Can you think of a similar event that you can choose to perceive as a gift of Love?

_____

_____

_____

_____

_____

_____

_____

_____

_____

_____

_____

_____

_____

_____

_____

February 26
"Where we love is home, home that our feet may leave, but not our hearts."
Oliver Wendell Holmes

Rene K

Rene phoned and asked when Jerusha's monthly pot luck was this month. I told her and she said she would like to go with me and could she bring a friend. Since it is open to all women and is a pot luck, of course, friends of friends of friends are welcome. Rene brought along Ellen who had written and published her own book and her partner also does the same. They live in my back yard, so to speak, since they live within a 3-mile distance from where I live. I would never have met them in my regular course of routines. How wonderful to meet a like-minded person and share her own spiritual quest and path on this earthly plane. This sharing of friends, too, is what Love looks like.

****

Can you think of a similar event that you can choose to perceive as a gift of Love?

_____

_____

_____

_____

_____

_____

_____

_____

_____

_____

_____

_____

_____

_____

February 27
"Unable are the loved to die, for love is immortality." Emily Dickinson

Brenda D

Brenda told me she and her husband did not give Christmas presents but gave presents whenever the mood struck them all throughout the year; however, one Christmas she gave me the most beautiful gift. After my near death experience, people felt I needed extra help (don't we all?) and I was gifted angels in various forms over the years. I had not gotten any for some years when Brenda gave me a beautiful little angel that lights up. It not only lights up, it also changes colours through the chakra range from red to white including seven colours in all. I think this little three-inch angel so reminds me of Brenda and her caring manner, that I shall name it Brenda, as well. Another shade of what Love looks like.

****

Can you think of a similar event that you can choose to perceive as a gift of Love?

_____

_____

_____

_____

_____

_____

_____

_____

_____

_____

_____

_____

_____

_____

_____

_____

February 28
"Love is what you've been through with somebody." James Thurber

Les O

Les has special talents when it comes to Photoshop photographs. Many people are reticent to share details of how they create masterpieces. Not Les. I asked what camera he would recommend and what photo-enhancing program he recommended. He immediately gave me all the details of what he uses including tips and suggestions for use. Sharing his knowledge is a special form of what Love looks like.

****

Can you think of a similar event that you can choose to perceive as a gift of Love?

_____

_____

_____

_____

_____

_____

_____

_____

_____

_____

_____

_____

_____

_____

_____

_____

_____

*February 29**
"Fashion your life as a garland of beautiful deeds." Buddha

Jon C

It seems that computer printers are made for obsolescence. I had one that worked great until the one-year warranty expired, then it quit. I asked Jon if he could recommend one that would not only give me good black-and-white text printouts, but would also print good colour photographs. He was very helpful in sharing his knowledge with pros and cons of different brands. I really appreciated this sharing and look on this as another form of Love, too.

****

Can you think of a similar event that you can choose to perceive as a gift of Love?

_____

_____

_____

_____

_____

_____

_____

_____

_____

_____

_____

_____

_____

_____

_____

_____

_____

_____

March 1
"Since love grows within you, so beauty grows. For love is the beauty of the soul."
St. Aurelius Augustine

Binnie L

In visiting ex-colleagues while talking generalities, I mentioned that I needed to replace my two outside storm doors and asked if Binnie might know someone who would do this for me. He immediately said he could and would do this if I got the doors. He suggested the brand and supplier of the doors and told me if I ordered them online instead of going directly to the outlet store, they would be cheaper. I did this. He stood behind his word and came and took off the old storm doors and installed the new ones. This was much more than I could ever think of doing myself. This is what Love looks like, too.

****

Can you think of a similar event that you can choose to perceive as a gift of Love?

_____

_____

_____

_____

_____

_____

_____

_____

_____

_____

_____

_____

_____

_____

_____

_____

_____

March 2
"Be loving and the love in your life will increase." Rhonda Britten

Andy D

When Andy's wife was dying of lung disease, he asked me if he could share his anguish at watching her demise at home via an email of his feelings. I was so unbelievably honoured to be asked to entrust such a fragile piece of his heart to my care. Of course, I immediately said 'Yes' and received such a genuine gift of his love for his wife and his sadness that she would be passing before he did that I tucked it away in the ethereal gold blue white gossamer-lined egg where I carry other people's cares for safe-keeping. This asking and giving is another example of what Love feels and reads like.

****

Can you think of a similar event that you can choose to perceive as a gift of Love?

_____

_____

_____

_____

_____

_____

_____

_____

_____

_____

_____

_____

_____

_____

_____

_____

_____

March 3

"You should love one another and behave lovingly because when love comes, everything comes. You should speak to one another with love and humility. Love is the essence."
Prem Rawat

Brad V

A friend suggested Brad as someone who would bring me a cord of wood at a reasonable price. I called and he immediately came to see where I lived, where I would want the wood dropped, and to collect the amount for the wood. Then, he never came again. I was so upset. How could this happen to me? I fretted, I told many people, I called repeatedly to Brad. He said he would come and bring the wood. He never did after many months and years. That money was not easily let go as it had many other places to be used; however, I now realize that Brad came in to my life to remind me about the art of letting go, of letting go of vengeance, of letting go of anger, of letting go of the victim mentality, of releasing those fear-based emotions that keep us shriveled, small and petty. I realize now that Brad came to help me remember to practice forgiveness and compassion with grace. He, obviously, needed the money even more than I did at the time and I thanked him in my mind for the opportunity to give it to him. This was not an easy lesson for me; however, I now know that this, too, is what Love feels like.

****

Can you think of a similar event that you can choose to perceive as a gift of Love?

March 4

"You will find, as you look back upon your life,
That the moments when you really lived
Are the moments when you have done things
in the spirit of love...." Henry Drummond

Lana I

After we retired, our lives took different directions and we didn't see each other unless one of us deliberately invited the other out for a tea to get updated on our lives. Lana and I would do this at least once a year even though we only lived a couple of miles from each other. This is how a life can be lived next to another and yet unless one looks correctly, it feels like the lives are not touching – but, they are. We are all energy, all one bowl of soup, and all our energy is always emmeshed with everyone else's. We just have to angle our perception a little differently to feel this. Lana would send me little emails that would always remind me we spent over twenty years together helping students find their way into the world of work through our courses. These emails have become little droplets of Love words on the cyber highway.

****

Can you think of a similar event that you can choose to perceive as a gift of Love?

_____

_____

_____

_____

_____

_____

_____

_____

_____

_____

_____

_____

_____

_____

_____

_____

March 5
"When you love someone, all your saved-up wishes start coming out."
Elizabeth Bowen

George C

I never got a newspaper delivered to my residence as I seemed to get the ink on my skin and clothes somehow. After I moved in to a duplex, I would come home from work and there would be a grocery bag hanging on my door handle with yesterday's newspaper in it. I would take it in and look through it, either with gloves on or from a distance, but I didn't know how it got on my door knob or who put it there. One day, when I was coming home a little earlier than usual, I saw the next door neighbour who had moved in to the other side of the duplex a couple of weeks before that, walking across the lawn from my door to his door and going inside his home. Aha! Now, I knew from whom and how the newspapers were coming. When I went to introduce myself and thank them for the newspapers, they chuckled and thought this was a great new adventure of theirs as to how to meet new people and pretended they did not put the paper there, but, of course, they did, and we had a great chuckle about it. We became great friends and helpers to each other over the next 15 years that they lived. This, too, is what Love looks like.
****

Can you think of a similar event that you can choose to perceive as a gift of Love?

_____

_____

_____

_____

_____

_____

_____

_____

_____

_____

_____

_____

_____

March 6

"The soul that can speak with its eyes can also kiss with a gaze." Author Unknown

Betty C

The phone rang on the Sunday morning about 9 a.m. It was my next door neighbour who lived on the other side of my duplex inside wall. Her bedroom was on the other side of the wall from my bedroom. She said, "Are you ok?" Of course I was ok and said so. She said you cried out last night about 3 a.m. for help. I am checking to see if you are ok. I had no recollection of the dream that I had called out from in need of help. She was checking on me. This concern is what Love sounds like.

****

Can you think of a similar event that you can choose to perceive as a gift of Love?

_____

_____

_____

_____

_____

_____

_____

_____

_____

_____

_____

_____

_____

_____

_____

_____

_____

_____

March 7
"If you would be loved, love and be lovable." Benjamin Franklin

Terry Z and Richard G

As I sat in the wheelchair looking out the living room window, my sister and youngest brother were crouched down on the ground planting the crocus bulbs that were sitting in the porch waiting to be planted after I came home from the hospital. They planted them in a fairy ring around the outside of the day lilies under the red maple tree, right in the centre of the lawn where I would be able to see them from the living room window when they came up through the snow the following Spring. While they were on their knees, my heart palpated with gratitude at their kindness. Another colour of Love.

****

Can you think of a similar event that you can choose to perceive as a gift of Love?

_____

_____

_____

_____

_____

_____

_____

_____

_____

_____

_____

_____

_____

_____

_____

_____

_____

_____

March 8

"My message of love is absolutely simple; nothing can be more simple than that."
Bhagwan Rajneesh

Angela P, Drew P, and Terry Z

At the end of the three-month mark of being wheelchair-bound with my broken leg, my first-born niece and her husband and my only sister stopped at my place on their way to my parents' place for Christmas dinner. I told them how I was using Mom's stationary bicycle to help my leg with therapy and that I had a 25-year old manual rower in the basement collecting dust. They immediately went to the basement and carried the very awkward and heavy rower up out of the basement. They got a bucket of hot soapy water and a rag and washed and wiped the equipment down. Then, they took it into my bedroom and set it up where I could access it. They then tried it out and had me see if I could get on and off and work it. All this caused them to be late to the dinner table on my behalf. This is also what Love looks like.

****

Can you think of a similar event that you can choose to perceive as a gift of Love?

_____

_____

_____

_____

_____

_____

_____

_____

_____

_____

_____

_____

_____

_____

_____

_____

March 9

"Love, you know, seeks to make happy rather than to be happy." Ralph Connor

Ian W

Through an inadvertent action, I was helped. Ian came and visited briefly while here seeing other friends. For whatever reason that I cannot remember, he had taken off his quilted, blue plaid vest and forgot and left it at my place. The day I drove up to the mail box and tried to stop my car from rolling down the hill by opening the moving car's door and trying to leap into it to put the brake on, I was wearing Ian's vest. When I was dragged down the uneven gravel and rock dirt hill hanging on to the car, with my legs under the car, the vest saved my upper and lower back from being shredded and burned by the friction. His inadvertent leaving of his vest saved me from further injury that day. This, too, is an example of Love.

****

Can you think of a similar event that you can choose to perceive as a gift of Love?

March 10
"Love is not what the mind thinks, but what the heart feels." Greg Evans

Sharon M-S

When I was in the ICU at the local hospital in Stage IV congestive heart failure, the head nurse came and said, "We're not supposed to allow any flowers in the Unit since there may be a patient who is allergic to one of them; however, since you are in a private room and there is a window sill, we will allow you to have this large cut flower arrangement in here for a couple of days." The flowers were really spectacular and reminded me of life and Summer. They were from my previous manager, Sharon, on behalf of all my ex-colleagues with whom I had worked for so many years, but – I knew they were really from Sharon. A bold, beautiful statement of caring and a lovely expression of Love.

****

Can you think of a similar event that you can choose to perceive as a gift of Love?

March 11
"To love is to receive a glimpse of heaven." Karen Sunde

Dr. Jonathan M

I came out of the farmer's market, got in my car, and drove forward, thinking it would be straight out to the paved road off the muddy gravel driveway. Not. I hit the paved, sloping curb with just enough momentum to slide over the top where my car then sat, hung up. I got out of the car just as Jonathan was taking boxes of wine out of the van and putting them on a dolly. I went over and introduced myself, telling him where we had met before, and could he help me get the car off the curb. He said he would help me after taking the dolly of boxes of wine into the market for his wife. In about 3 minutes he came back with another tall young man with him and they talked about whether they could drive the car off the curb. Nope. Just then, a group of students were coming down the road all dressed in green T-shirts. Jonathan commandeered them into helping and after 4 lifts of the car, pushing it sideways, the car was off the curb. Jonathan left so quickly I hadn't time to even say thank you. I sent him a card later. This is another lift of Love.

****

Can you think of a similar event that you can choose to perceive as a gift of Love?

_____

_____

_____

_____

_____

_____

_____

_____

_____

_____

_____

_____

_____

March 12
"A baby is born with a need to be loved and never outgrows it." Frank A. Clark

Leslen S

The saying is that men have their mid-life crises sometime in their 40s. Well, my mid-life crisis hit in my mid 40s, too. I wondered if I was doing exactly what I was supposed to be doing at the exact right time in my life and took a year off teaching to 'go see if I might find an answer to these questions'. I decided to take three months and drive across North America by myself, stopping every three to five days and visiting either a relative or friend as a way of keeping connected with people who reinforced my identity.

One such person was Leslen outside St. Louis, Missouri. I was careful to honour Samuel Johnson's statement about fish and guests starting to smell after three to five days and made it a point to leave a person's generosity and company before I started to stink, like fish might. When I was getting ready to leave Leslen's, she asked if I was going to the Grand Canyon. I said I didn't think I would stop on my way to California. She suggested I really would like the experience and if I was interested in staying overnight, she could make arrangements for accommodation as one had to book one year in advance for a hotel room inside the Park. She was friends with the Director of the South Rim of the Grand Canyon. I thought this a wonderful opportunity for a new adventure and took both she and the Director up on their offers. I am so glad that I had the experience of being shown around by the Director's ten-year old son and to actually hike on the trail down to the Colorado River at the bottom of the mile-long Grand Canyon trail. I am so honoured she offered and set up accommodation for me to have this experience. A totally unexpected and cherished gift of Love.

****

Can you think of a similar event that you can choose to perceive as a gift of Love?

_____

_____

_____

_____

_____

_____

_____

_____

_____

_____

_____

March 13

"The greatest happiness of life is the conviction that we are loved — loved for ourselves, or rather, loved in spite of ourselves." Victor Hugo

Maggie C

Maggie is my cousin. At the time of my North American trek to 'find myself', she was living in northern British Columbia. Although this was not on a regular route from the West Coast of North America back to the East Coast where I was living, I took the 100-Mile Highway up to see her as I had not visited with her for many many years.

She was totally gracious in having people in while I was there, touring me around the university where she was working, and generally feeding me and allowing me to get my laundry refurbished for the next leg of my quest. I feel this generosity on her part was a lovely act of Love that I still remember fondly.

****

Can you think of a similar event that you can choose to perceive as a gift of Love?

_____

_____

_____

_____

_____

_____

_____

_____

_____

_____

_____

_____

_____

_____

_____

_____

March 14

"Love takes off masks that we fear we cannot live without and know we cannot live within." James A. Baldwin

Gerald B

One day friends and I were at a property that I was getting ready to rent. It was in August and the field's grasses were dying down by that colour of hay that is so telling of the changing of the seasons. I got the idea that if I burned the patch of dried grasses, it would make the property look better. August is not the month to burn dried grasses. I found that out very quickly when a little breeze fanned the flames that were heading straight for the next door neighbour's house. My mind jumped into the barrel of Fear, big time, and I could see the fire taking out the entire mountain top of five miles to the brim of the Valley and all the inhabitants, animals, buildings, and, especially forests along the path.

Gerald was quick and got a shovel and rake and bucket and started turning over the burning sods to show that the fire had gotten below the surface level and was smoldering there, too. He and his companion and the neighbours – and the nearest fire department – got the fire under control after a couple of hours of really hard work. I am so appreciative of Gerald's quick thinking and actions. I am also so appreciative of fire fighters every where for their bravery and stamina. A colour of Love hard won.

****

Can you think of a similar event that you can choose to perceive as a gift of Love?

March 15
"Love is when you meet someone who tells you something new about yourself."
Andre Breton

Dr. Downey G

After six days in ICU, I was moved to a private room across the hall from the nurses' station. It was here a couple of days later that my uncle, Dr. Downey, hobbled in to my room to give me his beautiful, kind, loving gaze from his beautiful blue eyes, and his gentle words of encouragement as part of his magnificent bedside manner. He had phlebitis in his leg, which I am sure hurt most terribly, was at the hospital to see his own physician about his own issues, yet, he made time and effort to come and console me in my challenge to regain a foothold on life. His eyes and manner exuded so much Love, that all I could do was bask in that warm embrace.

****

Can you think of a similar event that you can choose to perceive as a gift of Love?

March 16
"Neither a lofty degree of intelligence nor imagination nor both together go to the making of genius. Love, love, love, that is the soul of genius."
Wolfgang Amadeus Mozart

Melvin D

Whenever Melvin would come to keep my general household clean and tidy, he would always ask what else he could do for me. Often, he didn't wait for a response, but would see something to do without asking. Putting some of the cords of wood lying in the driveway in to the basement and stacking it, was one of these gifts that he would bequeath me without bidding. This is what Love looks like, too.

****

Can you think of a similar event that you can choose to perceive as a gift of Love?

_____

_____

_____

_____

_____

_____

_____

_____

_____

_____

_____

_____

_____

_____

_____

_____

_____

_____

March 17

"The only reason we don't open our hearts and minds to other people is that they trigger confusion in us that we don't feel brave enough or sane enough to deal with. To the degree that we look clearly and compassionately at ourselves, we feel confident and fearless about looking into someone else's eyes." Pema Chodron

Debbie P

That almost three-week stay in hospital where I was still choosing whether to live or die was life-changing for me. There were so many people who came to the hospital on a daily basis that after about the third day, the head nurse in the intensive care unit came to me and said, "Who ARE all these people who are coming every day starting at 7:30 a.m. and are still ringing the bell to come in to see You at 10:30 p.m. at night?" I told her I was as surprised as she was. However, this outpouring of concern and rallying around showed me, in no uncertain terms, the power of love. Debbie brought watermelon, all cut up and ready to eat, as many times as I ran out of this delectable treat. This is also what Love tastes like.

****

Can you think of a similar event that you can choose to perceive as a gift of Love?

_____

_____

_____

_____

_____

_____

_____

_____

_____

_____

_____

_____

_____

_____

_____

March 18
"A good character is the best tombstone. Those who loved you and were helped by you will remember you when forget-me-nots have withered. Carve your name on hearts, not on marble." Charles Spurgeon

Glenne and Leander P
When I was in the intensive care unit of the local hospital in Stage IV congestive heart failure, many people who are in my family unit, my former colleagues, and my special friend support system all converged to shower me with their vigils of love. Glenne and Leander were one of the family units who came regularly to sit with my parents, to sit with me, to be there with their presence to let me know they were concerned about my life challenges and the look of concern in their eyes said I was Loved.

****

Can you think of a similar event that you can choose to perceive as a gift of Love?

March 19

"Love is a force more formidable than any other. It is invisible – it cannot be seen or measured, yet it is powerful enough to transform you in a moment, and offer you more joy than any material possession could." Barbara de Angelis

Cristy F

Over the years of teaching at the college and university level, there would be a student with whom I would have a 'sympatico' relationship. Cristy, unbelievably bright and gifted, was one such person over the years. For one so young, she was wise well beyond her years and we were able to share likes such as the radio station listened to most often, books read, and music. When she graduated, she gave me a package of her special music which was the Cowboy Junkies. I was stunned with this act of generosity and its implication that maybe I had made a positive difference in her life for a short period of time. I listen to their music and hear the sound of Love in their lyrics.

****

Can you think of a similar event that you can choose to perceive as a gift of Love?

_____

_____

_____

_____

_____

_____

_____

_____

_____

_____

_____

_____

_____

_____

_____

March 20
"The more I give to thee, the more I have, for both are infinite." William Shakespeare

Peter N

A friend's brother was between jobs when I needed someone to do some carpentry work and to hang some brocaded wallpaper at my house. I asked Peter if he was willing to come stay at my place and do the odd jobs that I wanted done. He came and did the most skilled work and would take almost no remuneration for his efforts. He stayed with me for the better part of a week during which time both his and my birthdays happened. We shared work, food, and talked about our lives. His willingness to share some of his life's experiences with me was special and I have never forgotten these talks of the telling of one's life's stories. This is what Love sounds like.

****

Can you think of a similar event that you can choose to perceive as a gift of Love?

_____

_____

_____

_____

_____

_____

_____

_____

_____

_____

_____

_____

_____

_____

_____

_____

_____

March 21

"No cord or cable can draw so forcibly, or bind so fast, as love can do with a single thread." Robert Burton

Lana I

Four of us retired all on the same day, two women and two men. Lana and I were from the same department and were feted by our department peers to a luncheon with a roasting of sorts afterwards. This included the telling of stories and pictures of us over the years showing us changing and, hopefully, maturing, as well.

I never thought to give a retirement gift to my other colleagues retiring the same year and day, but Lana did. She gave me the most beautiful iridescent humming bird hanging free-form on a wire from a base. I have put it on a window sill where I see it daily. Every time I look at it, I think of Lana and know this is another expression of Love.

****

Can you think of a similar event that you can choose to perceive as a gift of Love?

_____

_____

_____

_____

_____

_____

_____

_____

_____

_____

_____

_____

_____

_____

_____

March 22

"Being deeply loved by someone gives you strength, while loving someone deeply gives you courage." Lao Tzu

Max D

When I was strong enough to start reconnecting with people who I decided were important to my well-being in my life, I drove the hour and 20 minutes to visit with Max and Kelley. I am sure my hollowed-out cheek bones and bulging eyes were frightening to them to see when they would have remembered me so differently from the last time we had been together.

I was telling them that I was so cold all the time even though it was late Summer. That is an off-shoot of coming face-to-face with death – being cold, bone cold. I was saying this matter-of-factly, when Max got up, left the room and came back with a pair of his white heavy woolen socks. He insisted that I put them on and take them with me. I was in wonderment, which is where I spend a lot of my time since my near death experience – being amazed at the most loving acts being directed my way. This, too, is what Love feels like – a warm cloak of wool.

****

Can you think of a similar event that you can choose to perceive as a gift of Love?

_____

_____

_____

_____

_____

_____

_____

_____

_____

_____

_____

_____

_____

_____

March 23

"I always felt insecure and in the way, but most of all I felt scared. I guess I wanted love more than anything else in the world." Marilyn Monroe

Harold F

Anne and I were sharing ideas and concepts and she was in the dining room looking at my books. A knock came at the door. When I opened it, there stood my neighbour, Harold, holding a very large bag of the most delicious, delicate, rare, colourful Gravenstein apples – his own, home-grown. He gave me the bag of apples and visited with us, then left. How do you explain the taste of Love? Lovingly delicious.

****

Can you think of a similar event that you can choose to perceive as a gift of Love?

March 24
"Love is sharing your popcorn." Charles Schultz

Peter R

I don't remember how I met Peter and Jackie, but they sure made an impact on me.

They were living outside the safety of a regular job with a regular pay cheque, performing folk music around the province in different venues.

Peter introduced me to Carlos Castaneda's first book, "The Teachings of Don Juan." The book I still have was Peter's. Since then, I have acquired and read almost every book Castaneda wrote. His choice of word phrases have the ability to transport me to another reality just by reading the written word on the page.

I will never forget Peter's huge gift to me of opening up a whole new area of unknown but very relevant information to my questing mind. This is what Love reads like.

****

Can you think of a similar event that you can choose to perceive as a gift of Love?

_____

_____

_____

_____

_____

_____

_____

_____

_____

_____

_____

_____

_____

_____

_____

_____

_____

March 25

"You, as much as anyone in the universe, deserve your love and respect." Buddha

Daddy G

When my 6-month visit to the surgeon to see how my leg was healing and if I could start learning how to put weight on it and walk again, came up on my birthday, my Dad was the one to come with the car, get the wheelchair out of the house and into the car, get the walker down to the bottom of the steps, watch me hobble on one leg out onto the landing and watch me shinny down the 10 steps on my behind, then help me get into the car, take me to the hospital, help me get out of the car with the walker, get me in the wheelchair, and push me into the hospital, down the corridor, into the elevator, down the corridor to the waiting station to see the surgeon, then push me into the examining room. With good feedback, away we went again reversing the process with a stop in town where he helped me out of the car and into a hairdressing salon to have my hair cut, then out, back into the car, and finally back home shinnying back up the steps on my behind, and into the house and into bed exhausted from the experience. He did everything with grace and compassion, unbelievably patient at the process. My heart thanks him for this act of Love.

****

Can you think of a similar event that you can choose to perceive as a gift of Love?

_____

_____

_____

_____

_____

_____

_____

_____

_____

_____

_____

_____

March 26
"There is only one happiness in life, to love and be loved." George Sand

Alan C

The phone rang and it was Jerusha asking how I was doing. We talked for a bit, laughed some, shared WGO's (what's going on) in our lives, then she said the reason for the call. Alan had noticed when driving by my driveway that there were no car tracks in the snow. He wondered if I was ok, so Jerusha was calling to check in. This is what Love sounds like.

****

Can you think of a similar event that you can choose to perceive as a gift of Love?

_____

_____

_____

_____

_____

_____

_____

_____

_____

_____

_____

_____

_____

_____

_____

_____

_____

March 27

"Love is everything. It is the key to life, and its influences are those that move the world." Ralph Trine

Melissa M

Melissa practices reflexology, but not just any type of reflexology, she practices energy realigning and healing reflexology. When I had my first session with her, she lightly held my feet all the while talking with me. She never dug her fingers into my tender feet or ankles or lower legs or stretched my toes, she held my feet. After almost an hour of this pleasant experience, we were done. What really impressed me was the compassion and care that Melissa enfolded me in during this time. Who would think someone holding your feet could make you feel better in other parts of your body! This is what Love feels like, too.

****

Can you think of a similar event that you can choose to perceive as a gift of Love?

March 28
"Never self-possessed, or prudent, love is all abandonment." Ralph Waldo Emerson

Wayne I

I grew up with Wayne. He lived four houses up the road from where I lived. We went to the same two-room schoolhouse. His mother, an unhappy person, and our Primer to Grade 3 teacher, held him back one year so that we were in the same grade by Grade 3, even though he was a year older than I was.

When I moved to Toronto, Wayne was already living and working there. Being from the Maritimes, Maritimers are clannish in that they tend to seek each other out, especially when a long way from home territory with familiar people and surroundings. Wayne and I connected and one night went out to a movie. Since I had a car by then and he didn't, I picked him up and drove us to the movie, then took him back to his place afterward. This was the mid-1960s. At his place, he was fidgeting and not getting out of the car, so I turned off the engine and we talked a little bit. Finally, he said, "Should I kiss you goodnight?" I was shocked and said, No, that certainly was not necessary or expected. He heaved a great sigh of relief and got out of the car. You see, Wayne was gay and was always gay forever and we who grew up with him knew this. It was no big deal. It just was; however, since I had driven, he thought that it might be obligatory that he thank me somehow and all he could think of was giving me a kiss. His gentle consternation and consideration of how to thank me was an act of Love for which I am truly grateful.

****

Can you think of a similar event that you can choose to perceive as a gift of Love?

_____

_____

_____

_____

_____

_____

_____

_____

_____

_____

_____

_____

March 29

"We love in another's soul whatever of ourselves we can deposit in it; the greater the deposit, the greater the love." Irving Layton

Linda B

Linda was a breast cancer survivor of several years when one night at a social gathering she suddenly became teary-eyed. The people there were what I would label acquaintances, not what I would call friends; however, Linda shared that she had had a scare and that maybe the cancer was back. She was so overcome with fear that she needed the support of caring people around her just then to console her.

I considered this act of actively asking for help and support as a supreme gift of Love, maybe because asking for help is such a difficult task for me personally. I laud her bravery and courage in asking for what she needed when she needed it.

****

Can you think of a similar event that you can choose to perceive as a gift of Love?

March 30
"Love is that condition in which the happiness of another person is essential to your own." Robert Heinlein

Dennis and Toni C

The first air travel I did after my near death experience came five years later when I was saying, "I am ONLY five!" I really didn't know if I would have enough stamina and energy to do the airports, the security lines, the waiting, the walking. I parked my ego and vanity at the door to the airport and asked for wheelchair assistance from door to gate for each flight. The service was phenomenal.

When I arrived in Mexico, Dennis and Toni were waiting at the gate. They folded me in to their competent arms and from then on for the next week, they were never far from me. They took me to meet great people; fed me fantastic meals; booked me a condo a street away from their villa; took me to the tianguis; toured me around the villages by vehicle; taught me a new game to play; lavished me with historical and geographical facts about the place; and, generally, were the ultimate hosts – even though this is not their native home, but an acquired one. All this colourful scenery and cobblestone street-walking and tastes at the local eateries and the scintillating conversations with their newly-acquired friends, nurtured me into a completely safe feeling of being in a haven of Love.

****

Can you think of a similar event that you can choose to perceive as a gift of Love?

_____

_____

_____

_____

_____

_____

_____

_____

_____

_____

_____

_____

March 31

"To get the full value of joy you must have someone to divide it with." Mark Twain

Gini P

I met Gini on a nature walk in Kniffen Hollow. Isn't that a wonderful name for a dip in the ground? Kniffen Hollow! It reminds me of a Hobbit thought. Gini is passionate about wildflowers, photographs them, travels large distances, such as to Churchill near the Arctic Circle, to experience the blooming of special wildflowers. She then puts together the photographs, researches them and the geographic area where she was, and then shares these in talks to interested groups of people.

Having the gift of being in her company, hearing her adventure stories, seeing her pictures, going on a nature walk with her, these are what Love feels and looks and sounds like, too.

****

Can you think of a similar event that you can choose to perceive as a gift of Love?

_____

_____

_____

_____

_____

_____

_____

_____

_____

_____

_____

_____

_____

_____

April 1

"I believe in the compelling power of love. I do not understand it. I believe it to be the most fragrant blossom of all this thorny existence." Theodore Dreiser

Gordie W

My husband's great uncle was aged when I met him while in my 20s. He would have been in his 80s then. He was a kind, gentle man who was widowed. When he learned I knit, he gave me many of his wife's knitting magazines. These are for men's socks and men's vests and sweaters and women's dresses, sweaters, and children's knit outfits, too. All the knitting pattern magazines are from the 1930s and 1940s. I still have these books and look through them from time to time. It is a way that I remember Gordie's gift of Love to me.

****

Can you think of a similar event that you can choose to perceive as a gift of Love?

_____

_____

_____

_____

_____

_____

_____

_____

_____

_____

_____

_____

_____

_____

_____

_____

_____

April 2
"The greatest thing you'll ever learn
Is to love and be loved in return." Natalie Cole

Olivia Y

Another cousin came to see me when I was in congestive heart failure and in the intensive care unit of the local hospital. Being a nurse herself, she knew the limitation on bringing flowers to the Unit; however, she brought flowers anyway. And, the Unit nurse also allowed these to grace the window ledge in the room I was in. They were a reminder of all the summers I spent living for a couple of weeks at a time with her and her family, bathing in the galvanized tub straddling two wooden kitchen chairs; peeing in a pail in the girl's room and taking the slop bucket out in the morning; being teased by the boy cousins mercilessly; walking the two miles to the Bay of Fundy wharf at the shoreline and hanging around watching the fishermen doing their chores; picking wild strawberries for the strawberry shortcake dessert at suppertime; watching her mom, meaning my aunt, constantly baking in the wood stove, washing clothes on the hand scrub board, ironing clothes with the flat iron heated on the wood stove. All these memories were included in the flower bouquet Olivia brought to the hospital to remind me to choose life. This is what Love looks like, too, you know.

****

Can you think of a similar event that you can choose to perceive as a gift of Love?

April 3
"At the touch of love, everyone becomes a poet." Plato

Bob F

Another cousin's first husband had died and she was blessed with a second opportunity to share life with a retired military man named Bob. She died in her early 60s and Bob continued to be strongly connected to his second family unit.

One day he and I were visiting at his duplex and wild plants, in which both of us were interested, came up as a topic of discussion. He said that he had some wooded property that used to have a homestead on it, but now was 'way back in the woods'. He said there was a crop of horseradish and if I was interested he would take me to dig some up.

I thought this was a beautiful offer as Bob has Parkinson's and his gait and maneuverability were being challenged. His driving of the half-ton truck was ok and his walking seemed ok on the uneven ground – better than mine, actually. He had brought a spade and dug up some of the horseradish plant and we put it in a large plastic bag. I brought it home and replanted it. It has flourished. I have harvested and given roots away to others for their own culinary use. This, too, is what Love looks like.

****

Can you think of a similar event that you can choose to perceive as a gift of Love?

_____

_____

_____

_____

_____

_____

_____

_____

_____

_____

_____

_____

April 4
"If I know what love is, it is because of you." Herman Hess

Jamie G

A chance being at the right place at the right time gave me an idea for a raised garden bed – literally. I was driving by piles of discarded household items that university students had left for Spring cleanup by the waste management trucks, when I saw the wooden box that would have been used under a bed mattress as its form. I immediately thought of repurposing it as the beginning of a raised garden bed. I borrowed Dad's half-ton truck, got a friend and we went and collected it and brought it back to my place where we put it on the lawn face down.

I then called Jamie, who has a small farm with animals that make manure, and asked if he might bring me a load of manure to fill up my new garden bed. He not only brought the compost, filled the garden bed, but also brought seven nasturtium plants in their little burlap booties and planted each of them spaced around the raised garden bed.

He did not have to do this extra kindness; however, since he did, the nasturtiums have continued to reseed themselves every year, even though they are considered an annual and should only grow and bloom one summer then die away, giving me beautiful showy flowers and verdant trailing leaves year after year after year. The really big bonus of his gift is that nasturtium flowers, leaves, and seed pods are edible, highly nutritious, tasting a little like pepper, and an excellent source of Vitamin C. Who knew! Another gift of Love that keeps on giving.

****

Can you think of a similar event that you can choose to perceive as a gift of Love?

_____

_____

_____

_____

_____

_____

_____

_____

_____

_____

_____

April 5
"But I always think that the best way to know God is to love many things."
Vincent van Gogh

Dr. Russell G

We were having a regular kitchen bridge game at Mom and Dad's over the Thanksgiving season because a younger brother, Russ and his family, were home for a visit. So that each person has an opportunity to play with different people, after each rubber, then we switch partners. Russ and I were partners and I was not aggressive enough either in my bidding or in my playing. Russ took exception to this and tried to get me to realize just how important my bids and plays were to our success as a team. I tried to explain to him that I always play the best I can; however, I look on the game as just that – a game – and I get more benefit from being with my siblings doing something together than the winning or losing of point numbers on a piece of paper. He did not agree. We agreed to disagree.

At Christmas time, Russ and his family came home again, and, again, we played our traditional family kitchen bridge. During the couple of months' interval, Russ had thought about my point of view, and gave me a Christmas card that said he understood my point of view and he agreed that togetherness was much more important than the winning or losing of the game. I was so proud of him for realizing this really important life lesson. He showed how much maturity he has by putting his new-found wisdom on paper in a card to me (which I have kept). This is what Love reads and feels like.

****

Can you think of a similar event that you can choose to perceive as a gift of Love?

_____

_____

_____

_____

_____

_____

_____

_____

_____

_____

_____

April 6

"Love is the triumph of imagination over intelligence." H. L. Mencken

Dale G

I only knew Dale socially from seeing her around the campus when I was working, and casually at a couple of women's socials. It was a nice surprise when she phoned and said her identical twin sister was coming home to celebrate their birthdays and she was having a party. Would I like to come. What a gift. Of course, I would like to come. The food was mainly gluten-free which suited me just fine. Most of the guests knew each other and I knew some of them, as well. It was a lovely gathering. Dale inviting me to meet her twin and to share in their birthday party, is also what Love sounds like.

****

Can you think of a similar event that you can choose to perceive as a gift of Love?

April 7
"You can give without love, but you can never love without giving."
Robert Louis Balfour Stevenson

Mommy G

It took Mom many years to be comfortable with saying, "I love you" in words to us, her children. She did, however, show her love in many other ways. One of those ways was in the knowing what each of her five children especially liked for dessert choices and ensuring there were always a supply of these items whenever there was a special gathering. She was famous in the family for her home-made molasses cookies that took two days to make since the dough batter had to rest in the fridge overnight and in later years, she needed Dad's arms and muscles to do the mixing and rolling out as her shoulder ligaments had deteriorated too much. These molasses cookies were the size of saucers and she made them by the hundreds at a time. No small feat. Whenever one of us was leaving, there was often a cookie container of varying size offered as we went out the door to take with us. This is what Love tastes like.

****

Can you think of a similar event that you can choose to perceive as a gift of Love?

_____

_____

_____

_____

_____

_____

_____

_____

_____

_____

_____

_____

_____

_____

_____

April 8

"Remember, if you ever need a helping hand, you'll find one at the end of your arm... As you grow older you will discover that you have two hands. One for helping yourself, the other for helping others." Audrey Hepburn

Dr. Lois H

While recovering from the near death experience, I was seeing Dr. Lois, a Naturopath, who helped me tremendously. I really needed to find a medical practitioner who could write drug prescriptions who would honour my wishes of how to live and under what circumstances and I kept hoping that the Universe would give me a sign of what direction I should go in to find such a person.

After a little over a year on one of my frequent visits to see Dr. Lois, she casually said, "I wish you could get in to see Dr. Lisa, but she is not taking any more patients." There. The Universe had decided I was ready for the information I had been hoping for. I tucked that wish of Dr. Lois's away and did what I had to do to make it a reality. Dr. Lois's wish is another form of Love, for which I am truly grateful.

****

Can you think of a similar event that you can choose to perceive as a gift of Love?

_____

_____

_____

_____

_____

_____

_____

_____

_____

_____

_____

_____

_____

_____

April 9
"True love stories never have endings." Richard Bach

Philip DeB

When I was in the wheelchair for six months with the shattered leg healing, I had lots of time to do things that needed doing for many years. One of them was going through old files. In one file I found an old letter from 30 years ago that, I guess, could be thought of as a love letter, of sorts. It was a letter telling me why my decision to break off a relationship was faulty, even though the writer, Philip, was accepting my decision.

In rereading this letter 30 years later, I finally understood what Philip was telling me – and he was absolutely right – I was afraid of commitment and afraid to get hurt, so was constantly running from opportunities to be in a committed relationship. Had that letter not been saved, had my leg not been shattered, had I not been cooped up in the house in a wheelchair, then I would not have gotten around to finding the letter and rereading it – and, finally understanding its importance to my understanding about living in Love and not choosing Fear. Philip having the courage and taking the time to write that letter after our break-up, was an example of what Love sounds like.

****

Can you think of a similar event that you can choose to perceive as a gift of Love?

_____

_____

_____

_____

_____

_____

_____

_____

_____

_____

_____

_____

_____

_____

April 10

"We need 4 hugs a day for survival. We need 8 hugs a day for maintenance. We need 12 hugs a day for growth." Virginia Satir

Glenda H

One winter in my second time around, I was offered the opportunity to partake of a women's learning group using Christie Marie Sheldon's "I AM" material.

The group thought we would put on an International Women's Day workshop at the local community centre. As part of the planning and preparing, I asked the local grocery store manager if there would be a possibility of having some cheeses donated to make up a cheese plate. Glenda told me to pick out what I wanted and she would donate all of it. I picked out enough to make two large cheese trays, being willing to pay for at least one-half of the products. Nope. Glenda took the bill and I signed a chit and she donated the whole amount for the day's events. This was a larger sum than I ever thought would be donated by a local big-box grocery store as I know their markup is very small. This, too, is what Love tastes like.

****

Can you think of a similar event that you can choose to perceive as a gift of Love?

_____

_____

_____

_____

_____

_____

_____

_____

_____

_____

_____

_____

April 11

"Love is like water: We can fall in it. We can drown in it. And we can't live without it." Author Unknown

Edith I

Often we do not recognize when the Universe gives us a lesson in love and we only think about the emotional pain experienced during the initial part of the lesson. Often we never get past this emotional pain; however, sometimes we do.

Edith taught school to little people experiencing the system for the first time and for the next four years of their lives. She gave the impression she did not like kids. She picked on her own son in violent ways with rage in her actions. She beat, that is with the three-inch leather black strap, 1 ½ feet long, me the first day of school because I started colouring when she was saying the Lord's prayer. Now, I didn't know what she was doing or saying as I only, until then, knew the "Now I lay me down to sleep" prayer.

Although this was a violent way to start my school learning process, it and other traumatic experiences made me want to become a teacher myself so that I would not treat other learners I was entrusted with in a similar manner. You see, for every experience, there is a lesson – a lesson about Love. We just have to find the lesson and the meaning for our own lives and then live it.
****

Can you think of a similar event that you can choose to perceive as a gift of Love?

_____

_____

_____

_____

_____

_____

_____

_____

_____

_____

_____

_____

_____

April 12
"Life is the flower for which love is the honey." Victor Hugo

Heidi G

In casual conversation, I mentioned the work of Nicola Tesla and Wilhelm Reich on research into the biophysical properties of orgone which they believed enhanced life energy. Not only did Heidi, who I had no idea was interested in alternative healing therapies, know of Reich's work, she told me a story about the father of a friend of hers who had used an orgone product to revitalize his own 92-year old life. I was amazed that this casual conversation should lead to such an interesting information-sharing.

She then sent me information about where I could obtain an orgone accumulator product in the form of a 3 foot by 4 foot pillow to aid in healing. From this casual conversation, Heidi gave me another gift in the path to my healing. This is another feeling of Love.

****

Can you think of a similar event that you can choose to perceive as a gift of Love?

_____

_____

_____

_____

_____

_____

_____

_____

_____

_____

_____

_____

_____

_____

_____

_____

April 13

"He who experiences the unity of life sees his own Self in all beings, and all beings in his own Self, and looks on everything with an impartial eye." Buddha

Bob H

After college convocation, the custom of some groups of people was to convene at a local restaurant for a well-deserved luncheon and liquid libations for another year survived and thrived. Bob and I and another colleague decided to find an out-of-the-way place with fabulous food for the afternoon's reminiscences of the past year and to share some of what was going on in each of our lives, as well. Although we did this for one or two years in a row, then we didn't. It was Bob who resurrected the custom and we would always find a fourth who wanted to join our little group for some laughter and chatter. Bob wanting to continue these get-togethers and making the overture to make it happen, is also what Love sounds, tastes, and feels like.

****

Can you think of a similar event that you can choose to perceive as a gift of Love?

April 14
"To the query, "What is a friend?" his reply was "A single soul dwelling in two bodies."
Aristotle

Val D

Less than a year after my near death experience from untreated Graves' Disease and the resultant Stage IV congestive heart failure – and the fall and breaking of my dominant hand's wrist that was then in a cast for 9 weeks, I felt I really needed to do something to remind me that I was still alive.

What I did was book a 30-day trip by train across Canada, stopping here and there and visiting either family members or friends. My first stop was in Belleville, Ontario, where I was picked up at the train station by John and Val, two 89-year old friends of long standing. They were robust and had just sold their large house and rented another one where they were renovating the back yard to make it more like an English garden since they were originally from England. They really had no conception that they should have limitations because of their chronological age. It was the perfect place to start my new and what I call second life, with them as a reminder that all things are possible if only we choose to think them first.

They were the perfect hosts picking me up at the hotel every day and touring me around their neck of the woods, taking me to wonderful eateries, always to their place where perhaps John would play the piano, or we would just visit and chat.

The third morning when I was leaving and they picked me up to take me back to the train station, Val had gone specifically that morning to a local farmer's stand and gotten a fresh box of just-picked strawberries for me to take with me. This is what Love tastes like.

****

Can you think of a similar event that you can choose to perceive as a gift of Love?

_____

_____

_____

_____

_____

_____

_____

_____

_____

_____

April 15
"I believe that love cannot be bought except with love." John Steinbeck

Anna G

When a friend phoned and asked if I would like to help another person in her grieving process, I, of course, immediately said, 'Yes'. What I had the honour of participating in was a sacred ceremony for Anna whose husband had been tragically killed in an automobile accident and she was inconsolable. There were probably twelve women and we created a circle around Anna who lay on a sheepskin rug in the centre. We spent time reading chosen poetry to her, we let her fall backward into our arms, we cradled her, we wrapped her in our love. Then, we all ate a pot luck that ended the ceremony. I am so honoured to know Anna and to be allowed to help in her grieving and rehabilitation. Her openness to accepting a stranger into her home and to be part of this healing process, has changed my DNA from the outside in. This, too, is what Love feels like.

****

Can you think of a similar event that you can choose to perceive as a gift of Love?

_____

_____

_____

_____

_____

_____

_____

_____

_____

_____

_____

_____

_____

_____

_____

April 16

"Love is the voice under all silences, the hope which has no opposite in fear; the strength so strong mere force is feebleness: the truth more first than sun, more last than star." E.E. Cummings

Carol-Anne LoP

One of the intentions I had when I took the month-long train trip after my near death experience, was to see my birth daughter who lives in Toronto. When I was having lunch with her, she offered that if I wanted, I could come and meet her two children. As Carol-Anne and I have had a challenging time reuniting after her adoption, I was elated with this opportunity. Then, I was so saddened when I realized that I had already committed to attending a hockey game with my niece where her son was playing. I was also visiting and staying with my niece during this time and really felt that I would be insulting my host if I begged off to go see my two birth grand-children performing in synchronized swimming. So, I missed that opportunity; however, I am sure there will be another one. Carol-Anne offering this huge, gargantuan gift is definitely what Love looks like.

****

Can you think of a similar event that you can choose to perceive as a gift of Love?

April 17
"Conquer the devils with a little thing called love!" Bob Marley

Chandra L

After my near death experience, I was invited to a pot luck meal evening to meet some new people. I went along and had a very bad back muscle in crisis at the time. It was uncomfortable no matter what position I sat or stood in. This beautiful lithe person came over to me sitting in a chair, knelt down and wrapped her arms around my legs and rested her head on my knees. She looked up at me with such love streaming out of her eyes, I was mesmerized. She stayed this way for some time and I felt the pain lessening in my back, hips, and down the back of my legs. She then got up and moved on in the evening's activities. Her name is Chandra. She knows how to project Love and does so freely. I am so blessed I had her help that night.

****

Can you think of a similar event that you can choose to perceive as a gift of Love?

_____

_____

_____

_____

_____

_____

_____

_____

_____

_____

_____

_____

_____

_____

_____

_____

_____

_____

_____

April 18
"Love is the only flower that grows and blossoms without the aid of the seasons."
Khalil Gibran

Chris B

In my early 40s, I was back in school, specifically six weeks of summer school to learn the basics of teaching in a community college environment bringing a minimum of 10 years of working experience into the classroom. One of my colleagues, both at the institution where I worked, and attending the three-year summer school experience, was Chris. He would awaken us at 5:30 a.m. by learning how to play the bagpipes outside our windows. He and I also would walk morning after morning at 6 to 6:30 a.m. for close to an hour. On those walks around the town where we lived in residence, we talked about all sorts of life experiences, helping each of us to understand our own human lessons that came our way. This is what Love feels like, too.

****

Can you think of a similar event that you can choose to perceive as a gift of Love?

_____

_____

_____

_____

_____

_____

_____

_____

_____

_____

_____

_____

_____

_____

April 19
*"Love ever gives. Forgives outlives. And ever stands with open hands. And while it
lives, it gives. For this is love's prerogatives – to give, and give, and give."*
John Oxenham

Dennis C
Dennis and I started teaching at the local community college the same day, the same month, the same year, across the hall from each other – all 10 weeks after the college had convened the Fall semester; therefore, we were behind the eight ball, so to speak, and the students were feeling abandoned with multiple temporary teachers previously. Since we came to teaching from other careers, we were in our late 30s and early 40s. In order to increase our incomes, the system required time and education to move up the salary ladder. We could to nothing about time but put in the hours, days, months, and years. We could do something about the education.
We started taking university courses toward degrees that would be accepted by the college toward increases in salary. University was an hour's drive away and often we took the same courses to align our time spent in class. On these drives, we would sometimes talk about the course materials; however, many times we would talk about our life views and past experiences. I found these years of sharing mind-expanding and I look on these drives as a special gift of Love.
****

Can you think of a similar event that you can choose to perceive as a gift of Love?

_____

_____

_____

_____

_____

_____

_____

_____

_____

_____

_____

_____

April 20

"Spread love everywhere you go: First of all in your own house...let no one ever come to you without leaving better and happier. Be the living expression of God's kindness; kindness in your face, kindness in your eyes, kindness in your smile." Mother Theresa

Toni C

It was 9:30 in the evening of a Friday night. The phone rang. I picked it up and Toni was calling from Mexico. They had gotten my Christmas card after it roamed around trying to find them and she was phoning to say thank you. I had not talked with her for some years, really. We talked, mostly about their surprising discovery of Lake Chapala in the Mexico mountains where they are spending the Winter and how much they are enjoying the experience. We talked for at least an hour. She also asked if I might be interested in listening to the Esther and Gerry Hicks' CDs they had already listened to and wanted to regift. What a beautiful listening delight to hear her voice and for such a great length of time really hearing what they were experiencing and enjoying that Winter. This is what Love sounds like.

****

Can you think of a similar event that you can choose to perceive as a gift of Love?

_____

_____

_____

_____

_____

_____

_____

_____

_____

_____

_____

_____

_____

_____

April 21
"Love rules his kingdom without a sword." Proverb Proverbs

Dr. Leon M

After surviving the near death experience, a friend told me about an online metaphysical PhD program she was interested in taking. When I read the opportunities, I knew this was the coalition of all my years of seeking for answers to spiritual questions that I had had since a child. I immediately signed up and started the course. I felt that I had fallen into a cloud of soft, embracing warmth of understanding about all the disparate parts of my life to date. Dr. Leon's weekly spiritual programs were exactly what I needed at that time to help make sense of my life to date. I listened, nodding my head with an inward knowing that these words were my truth and they spoke my inner dreams in coherent words and sentences much better than I ever could. It is so wonderful when the Universe shows up with exactly what you need when you need it, even if you don't know what it is that you need. This, too, is what Love sounds like.

****

Can you think of a similar event that you can choose to perceive as a gift of Love?

_____

_____

_____

_____

_____

_____

_____

_____

_____

_____

_____

_____

_____

_____

April 22
"We must love one another or die." Jack Lemon

Eliz H

In my first year of the second life I have been gifted while I was still very weak and it was still iffy if I would recover enough to function, I got a phone call one evening from Eliz. It took some time for me to figure out who was calling as this was someone from my high school days with whom I played basketball and volleyball in tournament games.

She was calling to say that I must attend the 50th year reunion dinner at the local university. When I said I didn't think I had the energy to get dressed and go out for the evening, she said she would come and bring the 'team' to haul my body out of my house and to the dinner, if I did not show up by a certain time on my own. This insistence of the need for my presence is also what Love feels like.

****

Can you think of a similar event that you can choose to perceive as a gift of Love?

_____

_____

_____

_____

_____

_____

_____

_____

_____

_____

_____

_____

_____

_____

_____

_____

April 23
"Life without love is like a tree without blossoms or fruit." Khalil Gibran

Ferne MacL

When I was well on my way to actively dying from untreated Graves' Disease that put me in congestive heart failure, I had a little piece of heaven on the shore of the Bay. When I bought the land, it was covered with alder bushes so tightly packed it was very difficult to walk down through to the beach. Through asking around, I hired the nephew of a colleague to do what is called bush-wacking. This cut a swatch through the bushes; however, it left the roots with about 6 to 8 inches of alder trunk left in the ground which were dangerous to walk over and not conducive to driving over. I was telling all this to a colleague who offered to borrow her landlord's pick axe and lopers and come and dig and haul out roots for me. What? Who would want to do such labour-intensive back-breaking work, just for the exercise? Ferne would and did to my ever-lasting gratitude. This, too, is definitely what Love looks like as years later the path has still remained open and accessible to vehicles and feet. I am so grateful.

****

Can you think of a similar event that you can choose to perceive as a gift of Love?

April 24
"Friendship is the only cure for hatred, the only guarantee of peace." Buddha

Jerusha Y

One weekend Jerusha was having a shaman come to her place to help her do a journey with the objective of soul retrieval. She was to pick four to six other trusted persons to be part of the process to help her. When she asked if I might be available to join them, I looked on this as such a huge honour. Trusting someone with your soul is the most important action you can ever give someone else as a total gift of unconditional Love for which I am so grateful.

****

Can you think of a similar event that you can choose to perceive as a gift of Love?

_____

_____

_____

_____

_____

_____

_____

_____

_____

_____

_____

_____

_____

_____

_____

_____

_____

_____

April 25
"Love doesn't make the world go round. Love is what makes the ride worthwhile."
Franklin Jones

Charlie S

One door closes and another door opens. As my employment with a management consulting firm in Ontario was winding down, an opportunity to work with the Director of a local hospital rewriting almost a hundred job descriptions for the institution's different positions came into my life. Charlie was the Director and he and I became friends with that friendship lasting long after that couple of years' project. His life has taken many twists and jogs as mine has.

In the first year of what I call my new life, I took a train trip for 30 days across Canada getting off the train and staying with family and friends along the way for a couple days at a time. Even though it was many, many years since I had seen Charlie, his place was one of those stops. His wife was away for that long weekend; however, his culinary skills, his tour guide ability, and his reading library choices were excellent. He made me phenomenal meals, took me site-seeing around his area, introduced me to his work associates, and let me spend hours reading the story of his parents' escape from Nazi Germany during World War II. That weekend holds a special place in my memory. All of these sensations of taste, sight, sound, smell, and feel encompass what Love looks and feels and tastes like, too.

****

Can you think of a similar event that you can choose to perceive as a gift of Love?

_____

_____

_____

_____

_____

_____

_____

_____

_____

_____

_____

_____

_____

April 26

"The consciousness of loving and being loved brings a warmth and richness to life that nothing else can bring." Oscar Wilde

Sylvana C

Little things make up a life; they make the big things tolerable. When a recent acquaintance, who knew of my life-threatening challenges with congestive heart failure, asked how I had gotten better getting off the prescription drugs that I had left the hospital on, being told I would be on them for the rest of my life, I wasn't sure why she was asking. When she told me her mother was having problems with heart fluctuations and she was gathering as much information as she could to educate herself, I shared my story of where I had started, how I had gotten there (no experience is an accident – all are planned and intended soul journeys to learn about love), and how I had changed my life's direction. Her interest surprised me very much and her willingness to take the time to listen to my story is also what Love feels like.

****

Can you think of a similar event that you can choose to perceive as a gift of Love?

April 27

"If you have it, Love, you don't need to have anything else, and if you don't have it, it doesn't matter much what else you have." James M. Barrie

Dee

In my new lease on life, I tried my hand at growing my own vegetables. Since I like cucumbers, I tried growing them. My objective is always to not use chemical fertilizers or chemical pesticides since my attitude this second time around is to stay as healthy as possible for the time I am here. My little cucumber seeds would grow these exquisite fragile two-leaf protuberances on the little stems and I would send them happy thoughts when I saw them. Within a day or two the little leaves would be gone from the stem. I was so disappointed.

So, I did my homework and found that the culprit was probably cut worms who liked them as much as I did. A suggestion was to sprinkle dried, crushed, cooked egg shells around the plants to deter the worms. I thought of the little bistro where my cousins and I go to celebrate each other's birthdays. I asked Dee if she would save me her egg shells from the bistro. She did. Boy, did she save me egg shells. It was a great supply. Her life is hectic and full. Having to add another request to remember to do to her 'to do' list was probably burdensome; however, she did it. This, too, is what Love looks like.

****

Can you think of a similar event that you can choose to perceive as a gift of Love?

_____

_____

_____

_____

_____

_____

_____

_____

_____

_____

_____

_____

_____

April 28
"Love does not dominate; it cultivates." Johann Wolfgang von Goethe

Dr. Tom McE

One night around Christmas the phone rang after 8 p.m. When I answered it, there was a voice from the distant past – Dr. Tom. We caught up on what was happening in our lives over the last 30 years and that was that – or so I thought.

A couple of weeks later, the phone rang again on a Saturday night and, again, it was Dr. Tom. This continued for almost two years. I enjoyed hearing about his research and what travels he had been doing. It reminded me of an earlier time in my life living in the big city.

Dr. Tom and his wife had taken me in when my marriage failed and had nursed me with kindness all those years ago. Now, it felt that Dr. Tom needed some nursing of his own that he perhaps got through these, sometimes, weekly phone calls. I'll never know; however, I know that him calling on me to fill some type of void in his life at the time is another voice of what Love sounds like.

****

Can you think of a similar event that you can choose to perceive as a gift of Love?

_____

_____

_____

_____

_____

_____

_____

_____

_____

_____

_____

_____

_____

_____

_____

_____

April 29
"People are unreasonable, illogical, and self-centered. Love them anyway."
Mother Teresa

Gerry F

Why Gerry started doing wood-working in his basement with an active vice-principalship position, I don't know. What I do know is that he made a beautiful cane and gave it to me. He could never know how valuable that cane has been and is with my damaged leg. A gift that didn't need service until 15 years later. Perhaps Gerry is prescient? I thank him very time I see the cane hanging there ready to help. Another demonstration of Love.

****

Can you think of a similar event that you can choose to perceive as a gift of Love?

_____

_____

_____

_____

_____

_____

_____

_____

_____

_____

_____

_____

_____

_____

_____

_____

_____

April 30
"Woe to the man whose heart has not learned while young to hope, to love - and to put its trust in life." Joseph Conrad

Cindy H and Rick O'R

Not having children or a spouse to celebrate Christmas holidays for and with means that I gravitate toward those who do celebrate in loving ways. For several years, I was included for the Christmas dinner at my life-time friend's daughter's place. Cindy and Rick were gracious in accepting me into their large extended family grouping as one of them. I'm not sure they realize how much these get-togethers mean to me. I know they were the smell and taste of Love, freely given.

****

Can you think of a similar event that you can choose to perceive as a gift of Love?

_____

_____

_____

_____

_____

_____

_____

_____

_____

_____

_____

_____

_____

_____

_____

_____

May 1

"Love yourself first and everything else falls into line. You really have to love yourself to get anything done in this world." Lucille Ball

LaVerne P

It is always the little things that have great meaning. I had a favourite vest and the zipper broke in it. I found another zipper online and got it. I then tried to install the new one taking out the old one first. I wasn't doing very well at this so I asked LaVerne if she would do it. Now, you must understand sewing is one of LaVerne's passions, so I had gone to the best with my request. I knew that she always had multiple projects on the go at any one time and many of them with deadlines. She had no qualms about saying that she would put the new zipper in for me, which she did. Every time I put the vest on, I think of her. This, too, is what Love looks like.

****

Can you think of a similar event that you can choose to perceive as a gift of Love?

_____

_____

_____

_____

_____

_____

_____

_____

_____

_____

_____

_____

_____

_____

May 2

"Parents must get across the idea that I love you always, but sometimes I do not love your behavior." Amy Vanderbilt

Mommy G

At one point my good leg and foot was in crisis and I was pretty much house-bound. I had not been out to see my parents for 2 weeks even though it is only a 20-minute drive from my place. Mom had been home for 4 weeks now from being in the hospital in congestive heart failure. The phone rang one Thursday morning and it was Mom asking if there was anything she could go out and get and bring me at my house, even though there are 10 steps on the outside of my house to get inside. I was so overwhelmed with this act of kindness, I was feeling love pouring into my heart. Even though her health was compromised, she reached out to offer help to me. This is also what Love looks like.

****

Can you think of a similar event that you can choose to perceive as a gift of Love?

_____

_____

_____

_____

_____

_____

_____

_____

_____

_____

_____

_____

_____

_____

_____

_____

May 3
"All the beautiful sentiments in the world weigh less than a single lovely action."
James Lowell

Nancy B

I met Nancy at the monthly women's pot luck salon. She brought the tastiest home-made cracker I had ever tasted. Since my near-death experience and the Divine intervention of suddenly ceasing the smoking of cigarettes after 40 years, my taste buds were rejuvenated re-experiencing all sorts of delicacies. These crackers were in that category of delicacy. I asked Nancy if she would share her recipe. Within a day an email came in with the recipe in it. Many people are reticent to share trade secrets from which they get notice. Not Nancy. She gave the whole recipe without leaving anything out plus instructions. This, too, is what Love tastes like.

****

Can you think of a similar event that you can choose to perceive as a gift of Love?

_____

_____

_____

_____

_____

_____

_____

_____

_____

_____

_____

_____

_____

_____

_____

_____

_____

_____

May 4

"Can miles truly separate us from friends? If we want to be with someone we love, aren't we already there?" Richard Bach

Jerusha Y

When I turned 65, my former student, my present osteopath/masseuse, life-saver, friend-in-the-making, asked me to come for breakfast at 8 a.m. She made scrambled eggs with Ezekiel English muffins with special jelly, pomegranate/nectar juice, Bodum-pressed coffee. This was the day I was booked to have an osteo/massage treatment. After breakfast and catch-up talk, she asked me if I would like to do a session of QiGong, which I had introduced her to. Of course, I said 'yes'. Then, she gave me the most thorough, deep, intense, wonderful treatment for almost an hour and a half. By now it was 11:30. She then asked me if I had time to stay for lunch. Of course, I did. She had arranged with her husband, Al, beforehand, that he would get some sushi and bring it to us for lunch, which he did. We had lunch and more exchanging of ideas and watching the birds on her deck. She then told me that she wanted to give me something special for my birthday and could not think of anything that she felt would do, so she gave me her time instead. I left there at 1 p.m. What a phenomenal birthday present! Better than any material item could ever be. I love her. This is what Love looks like, feels like, tastes like, sounds like, too.

****

Can you think of a similar event that you can choose to perceive as a gift of Love?

_____

_____

_____

_____

_____

_____

_____

_____

_____

_____

_____

_____

_____

May 5

"When you have nobody you can make a cup of tea for, when nobody needs you, that's when I think life is over." Audrey Hepburn

Marj H

Growing up in a small village, I felt everyone seemed to know everything about everyone else. At that time, I found this invasive and unnerving. Today, after living in the same place for more than 16 years, I now understand the concept of community.

Marj lives next door. She and her husband are my neighbours. We look out for each other. On one Easter weekend, Marj arrived at my door with homemade treats. We shared a cup of tea and some of the treats while sharing what was happening in our lives. When she left, she leaned in and gave me a kiss. This is what Love feels like.

****

Can you think of a similar event that you can choose to perceive as a gift of Love?

_____

_____

_____

_____

_____

_____

_____

_____

_____

_____

_____

_____

_____

_____

_____

_____

May 6
"Who so loves believes the impossible." Elizabeth Barrett Browning

Angela Z

It was February 14, Valentine's Day. Whether it was the hypothyroidism or my failure to reach out, I was feeling a little left out of the celebration of Love day. Then, an email came in. It was an e-card telling me I was loved from Angela. The timing was perfect. I needed that and there it was. I just didn't know who would be filling my need. This is what Love sounds like, too.

****

Can you think of a similar event that you can choose to perceive as a gift of Love?

_____

_____

_____

_____

_____

_____

_____

_____

_____

_____

_____

_____

_____

_____

_____

_____

_____

_____

May 7

"To be loved for what one is, is the greatest exception. The great majority love in others only what they lend him, their own selves, their version of him."
Johann Wolfgang von Goethe

Lora S

Sometime in the 1990s, Lora sent me the most wonderful birthday card. It was as large as this page and on the front there was a poem by Jenny Joseph called, "When I Am Old I Shall Wear Purple." The inside was blank and Lora had written a little update – a snapshot of what was happening at that time in her life.

I liked the card so much that six weeks later on her birthday, I also wrote a little update note and sent it along.

It has now been more than 20 years that this card has been back and forth from Oklahoma to Nova Scotia. We have added more purple pages to the centre on which to write our little update notes. Sometimes a birthday has gotten missed and there is no little note. This card is still wending its way back and forth every March and May through the regular, snail-mail postal services. This, too, is what Love looks like.

****

Can you think of a similar event that you can choose to perceive as a gift of Love?

_____

_____

_____

_____

_____

_____

_____

_____

_____

_____

_____

_____

_____

May 8
"Where love reigns the impossible may be attained." Indian Proverb

Priya N

How do those significant people come into your life? Usually, I don't know the details of how something comes about. With Priya, I do. After being diagnosed with osteoporosis and the specialist putting the fear of God into me, I decided that my life and my body was my responsibility and I needed to learn, learn as much as possible about this diagnosis of brittle bones. I joined a website blog called 'The National Osteoporosis Foundation' located in the United States with followers and bloggers from all over the world sharing questions and findings and thoughts and success stories. I found this site at the right time in my learning journey. Priya lives in India at the foothills of the Himalayas. He studied in the United States earlier in his career. He poses relevant questions about research into possible aids for reducing the effects of osteoporosis. He and I shared communication and he let me know of his other side from his scientific abilities, that being as an artist, an artist who makes home-made comedy skits and videos them. I went to his website and watched several of his skits. They are priceless and do exactly what they are intended to do. Make one laugh at oneself. How better to share another form of love. A perfect outlet for Love.

****

Can you think of a similar event that you can choose to perceive as a gift of Love?

May 9

"When two people relate to each other authentically and humanly, God is the electricity that surges between them." Martin Buber

George C

It was Christmastime a year after the car accident that did so much harm to my body. Going to see George was a 30-minute drive one way. He lived in an apartment in a health facility where he was pretty much independent. When I walked in to his apartment, he was making a turkey dinner for us to share. He was mostly confined to a wheelchair by now at age 90 with difficulty walking. From this wheelchair, he was cooking a traditional Scottish Christmas dinner as best as he could to share with me.

I was overwhelmed with feelings of surprise and gratitude for this immense expense of energy on his part for me. This definitely is what Love looks, smells, and tastes like.

****

Can you think of a similar event that you can choose to perceive as a gift of Love?

_____

_____

_____

_____

_____

_____

_____

_____

_____

_____

_____

_____

_____

_____

_____

"Love is an act of endless forgiveness, a tender look which becomes a habit."
Peter Ustinov

Jerusha Y

How large a heart is shown when someone says, "I think you can get more help with someone else." Jerusha has done this. She recommended that I see a bodywork masseuse who could work on deep-seated trauma that my body has been compensating for by misaligning my muscles and tendons and ligaments, and ultimately bones, where I experience pain because of these compensations in how I sit and lie and stand and walk. Only someone without personal ego, with a larger-than-normal heart, someone who is genuinely wanting to help each contact to be a healer and to be healed. This is a heart-felt expression of Love.

****

Can you think of a similar event that you can choose to perceive as a gift of Love?

_____

_____

_____

_____

_____

_____

_____

_____

_____

_____

_____

_____

_____

_____

_____

_____

May 11
"Music is only love looking for words." Lawrence Durrell

Doug G

After we four women tied down two tarps duck-taped together over the travel trailer, ends still flapped whenever the wind blew leaving the broken vent on top potentially open for rain to get in. Then Doug came. He hauls things in trucks and knows about tying down tarps. Within about 20 minutes, compared to our hour and one-half's efforts, he had taken the tarps off and put them back on and tied them down – right. They stayed on until the trailer was sold, over a year later, with no detrimental rain or snow getting inside. This is what Love looks like, too.

****

Can you think of a similar event that you can choose to perceive as a gift of Love?

_____

_____

_____

_____

_____

_____

_____

_____

_____

_____

_____

_____

_____

_____

_____

_____

_____

_____

May 12
"It is easy to halve the potato where there is love." Irish Saying

Kathy R

After the accident and my move from the hospital to my home bedroom, therapy was to be continued as it had been started the day after the surgery in the hospital so that the knee and leg and ankle and foot would not have a chance to forget their roles in my life. I had been asked at the hospital when I was being gotten ready for discharge who I might like to contact regarding physiotherapy. Since I had been to a therapist near my home in previous years, I told them I would like to ask Kathy if I could get help from her. That was that. After a day or two at home adjusting, my sister took a call from Kathy asking when I could come for a therapy session. I told her that if I came to her practice I would have to hire the ambulance and paramedics to come get me out of the house and bring me back again after therapy. She said that would not do. Within an hour she was at my house, crawling up on my bed with me, taking my leg out of the removable cast, examining it, testing it, moving it, and writing out a routine for me to start doing right away. She came three times a week and continued this care for six months. I would never have believed this kind of service is available. I can walk today partly because of this professional yet personal expression of Love.

****

Can you think of a similar event that you can choose to perceive as a gift of Love?

_____

_____

_____

_____

_____

_____

_____

_____

_____

_____

_____

_____

_____

May 13

"We are formed and molded by our thoughts. Those whose minds are shaped by selfless thoughts give joy when they speak or act. Joy follows them like a shadow that never leaves them." Buddha

Daddy G

The mackeral truck was at the usual place on that Thursday morning. I got two bags of tinkers and headed home with them on ice. A call out to Mom and Dad's place to check if Dad was available and away I went with my catch. A quick slice under the top gill and down on a slant toward the head across the neck, turn the fish over and slice the head completely off under the other side's gill and down into the neck. Then, take the scissors and cut a V out of the neck on the belly side. Now, take the scissors and slice just under the skin down the belly. Clip off the tail. Take your fingers and slide them down the back bone of the fish to take out the entrails. Wash under cold water and voila! a beautiful gift from the ocean. Dad cleaned over 25 mackeral for me. I gave him some and brought the rest home to freeze for the winter. Another smell of Love.

****

Can you think of a similar event that you can choose to perceive as a gift of Love?

_____

_____

_____

_____

_____

_____

_____

_____

_____

_____

_____

_____

_____

_____

_____

May 14
"The life and love we create is the life and love we live." Leo Buscaglia

Alex P

You know you meet someone at someone's home and you think 'that person has a kind demeanour', well, I met Alex in such an environment. I knew she was a very good artist, was a masseuse, had a dog, had a partner, had recently moved houses. What I didn't know was her generosity. We were talking about shampoos one night at a pot luck and I was saying how difficult it was to find shampoo without parabens. She said she bought her locally-made soap from a farmer's market and that the soap was not only good for hands and face and body washing, but was also good for shampooing hair. I was surprised to hear this as I could remember using hard bar soap as a young person when there was no liquid shampoo and it leaving my hair with a white sticky goo in it that made it impossible to brush or comb. She said, yes, this soap could be used as a shampoo and she used it. That was a nice piece of information to know. I just didn't know from which farmer's market she got the soap. I got her phone number and phoned and left a message asking her to tell me where she got it or from whom. Time passed. A couple of weeks went by and I got a call saying she had put the message in a pant pocket where it had gotten forgotten and here she was returning my call and she would be going to the farmer's market that Wednesday afternoon and would I like her to pick up a bar of the soap? Of course, I said yes, thank you, I would appreciate that very much. It is these tiny little kindnesses that make up a great big bowl of Love.

****

Can you think of a similar event that you can choose to perceive as a gift of Love?

_____

_____

_____

_____

_____

_____

_____

_____

_____

_____

_____

May 15

*"Animals are reliable, many full of love, true in their affections, predictable in their
actions, grateful and loyal. Difficult standards for people to live up to."*
Alfred Montapert

Tigger

Never underestimate the power of love. Friends were moving and their cat was not able to travel. Too emotionally upsetting for him. I agreed to adopt him. He hated being abandoned and it took several years for him to accept his new accommodations and owner. But, when he did, boy, did he step up to the plate well!

One November I got a stomach illness that would take me to my knees and to my bed not being able to breathe with so much pain that would pass after a day or so only to come back again. This went on for 6 weeks until it passed. I did not seek professional help for a variety of reasons, but...Tigger was noting my inability to get out of bed for periods of time and would sometimes come and get up on the bed and lick my hand or foot if it was outside the covers.

One Friday evening I was well enough to be up and on the living room couch watching TV while doing laundry in the basement, going back and forth from washer to dryer. About 10:30 p.m. Tigger came in to the living room and sat and mewed with eyes all queer like he was trying to make love to me or something. I heard the washer stop and jumped up to go to the basement and change the clothes to the dryer. Tigger was right beside my left leg, mewing all the time. I got to the head of the basement and saw a shadow at the bottom. I thought oh, oh, maybe a raccoon or skunk has come in through the cat door in the screen and is now in the basement. I went down slowly. At the bottom was a cock pheasant – dead. Tigger went over and sniffed it and mewed again. I looked for blood. There was none, just two little pricks in the back of the neck. I know Tigger caught this and brought it in through the cat door. I think he brought it as a gift to help me get better. This is what Love does.

****

Can you think of a similar event that you can choose to perceive as a gift of Love?

_____

_____

_____

_____

_____

_____

_____

_____

_____

_____

May 16
"Do not wish to be anything except what you are." St. Francis

Wanda and Binnie L

Also during the 6 weeks that I was so sick that November, a colleague and his wife brought care packages by the box full. Binnie hand made chicken soup. Wanda made rolls, muffins. These they would bring and leave on the kitchen table for me.

Whenever I heated up the chicken soup, the smell was so healing all I could think about was the infinite variety of what Love smells like.

I am sure these 'fowl' smells must have influenced Tigger's later behaviour to which I attribute anthropomorphic motivations.

****

Can you think of a similar event that you can choose to perceive as a gift of Love?

_____

_____

_____

_____

_____

_____

_____

_____

_____

_____

_____

_____

_____

_____

_____

_____

May 17
"One word frees us of all the weight and pain of life: that word is love." Sophocles

Daddy G

I had this idea that I wanted a wild, beautiful Mexican hand-painted sink to enjoy. When the centre drain in the original ceramic main bathroom sink started leaking, I asked Dad to help me design a new counter to hold a Mexican hand-painted sink.

We spent some time measuring, drawing, re-measuring, re-drawing, and re-measuring again. He had his own business doing plumbing, heating, and wiring for over 50 years. By now he was in his mid-80s. But, his age has never stopped him from solving problems and trying new things. There was not a lot of room between the toilet and door so Dad wanted to maximize the usage for both a man standing up using the toilet and a woman sitting down with knee room. All these needs had to be taken under consideration in the design.

Once all the requirements were looked after, Dad physically came to my house, and installed the counter and holder for the sink, installed the sink, hooked up the plumbing and tested it all out. It works beautifully. I painted it all up and enjoy the calla lilies in the bowl of the sink every time I use it. This, too, is what Love consists of.

****

Can you think of a similar event that you can choose to perceive as a gift of Love?

_____

_____

_____

_____

_____

_____

_____

_____

_____

_____

_____

_____

_____

May 18
"The love we give away is the only love we keep." Elbert Hubbard

Linda B

Multiple times I have found an item that I wanted to buy on the Internet; however, the company could or would not ship it to Canada.

In the 1980s I was working in Oklahoma at American Airlines and met a wonderful person living in Dallas, Texas at the time, who was also working for American Airlines, too. She and I have remained long-distance friends for more than 30 years. I have not seen her for at least 15 years; however, we are connected – somehow.

When I decide that I would really benefit from the item that I would like to purchase off the Internet but the company does not ship to Canada, I ask Linda if she would be willing to have it shipped to her and then for her to readdress it to me and I would pay her for the extra postage. She has always said 'yes'. I consider this an act of Love on her part. I get it and I Love her for this.

****

Can you think of a similar event that you can choose to perceive as a gift of Love?

May 19
"Love is not blind; it is an extra eye, which shows us what is most worthy of regard."
James M. Barrie

Debbie P

At some point in my downward trajectory toward death, I had been spending most of my days and nights half-lying on the couch watching cartoons on TV. Since I couldn't breathe with the buildup of fluid retention, I had to be in a 'semi-reclining' position to sleep while still trying to get some breath. I found the YTV channel and became intrigued with the story line embedded in the "Land Before Time" series about a group of childlike dinosaurs and their experiences learning the big lessons in life through tribulations.

I mentioned these to Debbie and how interesting I was finding them. She said she and her daughter had the whole set on VHS and DVD and loaned them all to me. I spent weeks watching these, forgetting that I was actively dying at the same time. This loan of exactly where I was in my soul's journey of abdication and ignoring, allowed me to not be stressed with my deteriorating health, which, in retrospect was exactly what I needed to be doing at the time. This, too, is what Love looks like.

****

Can you think of a similar event that you can choose to perceive as a gift of Love?

_____

_____

_____

_____

_____

_____

_____

_____

_____

_____

_____

_____

_____

May 20
"The only love worthy of a name is unconditional." John Powell

Jennifer McL

I have no recollection of how I fell into listening to webinars on health and spiritual topics, but I do know the name of the first coordinator of such a gift. It was Jennifer.

Jennifer has the most appealing ability to sing her heart song a cappella that is very powerful. I fell into these webinars of speakers such as Greg Braden, Carol Look, Norm Shealy and so many others that had information for me that was needed at exactly the right time in my life. Divine works so beautifully for our ultimate good.

If Jennifer had not offered these webinars free when I was house-bound either in a wheelchair or too weak to be out and about, then I would never have been attracted to all the other webinar coordinators that have continued to offer information and knowledge relevant to my learning at this point in my life. This is what Love sounds like, too.

****

Can you think of a similar event that you can choose to perceive as a gift of Love?

_____

_____

_____

_____

_____

_____

_____

_____

_____

_____

_____

_____

_____

_____

_____

May 21

"For every beauty there is an eye somewhere to see it. For every truth there is an ear somewhere to hear it. For every love there is a heart somewhere to receive it."
Ivan Panin

Anne M

Anne had mentioned the bodywork practitioner and intuitive counselor that she frequented several times. On a visit to her place, she said she had decided that she would like to take me with her to a combined session where we alternated with the two practitioners and since it was some distance away and tucked into a sea cove, she would go so that I would not have trouble finding it. What a gift. My requirement was to phone the number on the brochure she gave me and to make an appointment. She said they were very busy and often booked for more than 6 months at a time. I phoned and left a message saying that I was a friend of Anne's and that we would like a combined session. I got a return message a week later with a date and time. The date and time would be during the first week of Anne's return to teaching. I mentioned all this to our masseuse who said she would be very interested in going if possible. I called Anne and left a message that if she was unable to go on the appointed date and time, then Jerusha would be interested in taking her place. A while later, Anne, who had initiated this opportunity for me, who had given me access to her contacts, who had graciously offered to drive me, then phoned and left a message that she would probably be very tied up at work on that day and that she felt Jerusha was to have her spot so that the two of us should go instead. This is what Love looks like, too.

****

Can you think of a similar event that you can choose to perceive as a gift of Love?

_____

_____

_____

_____

_____

_____

_____

_____

_____

_____

_____

May 22
"Happy are those who dare courageously to defend what they love." Ovid Ovid

Margaret FW

Margaret was my neighbour across the street who befriended me after I shattered my leg and was in a wheelchair in my home for six months. One March Saturday at the very beginning of Spring, she called and asked if I would like to go for a little drive up in to her son's apple orchard to see where their original New England Planter land grant was situated. Of course I was available and interested in the outing. It was about 3:30 in the afternoon when we left in her car. She was 20 years my senior, but she never accepted age numbers as having any relevance to how one lived. We stopped at the pond and watched two male ducks squabble over the attention of one female duck. We stopped at a clearing where robins stayed all winter in a protected place. We went through one orchard and she decided that rather than turning around and retracing our drive, she would continue on up a little grade and around another orchard section to make a loop back to the barn and houses. That little grade. The soil was a water-clogged clay mixture that grabbed on to the car's wheels and sucked them in to a locked position. Margaret was a pioneer who did not have defeat or 'no' in her vocabulary. We tried to get that car unstuck for almost two hours, carrying twigs and rotten sticks and dried grasses from the edges of the fields to push under the tires. We used the cat litter she had in the trunk of the car to no avail. We pushed. We strategized. We even used the rear seat footwell rubber mats, also to no avail. One is still up there at the back of the orchard years later. It was never retrieved. Finally, the sun was going down and we were cold. We bundled up and took a leisurely walk back down to her son's house where she handed the car keys to her daughter-in-law and asked that someone take the tractor or half-ton truck up and bring her car home. This adventure was on my 65th birthday. I loved the whole experience and kept thanking her for the wonderful gift. This, too, is what Love looks like.

****

Can you think of a similar event that you can choose to perceive as a gift of Love?

_____

_____

_____

_____

_____

_____

_____

_____

_____

May 23

"The day will come when, after harnessing space, the winds, the tides, and gravitation, we shall harness for God the energies of love. And on that day, for the second time in the history of the world, we shall have discovered fire." Pierre Teilhard de Chardin

Vicki D

A colleague gave me a cute little birthday card on my 50th birthday that I felt was appropriate to the both of us. So…on her birthday two months to the day from mine, I sent the card back to her. She liked the idea so much that the card has been back and forth between us now for almost 20 years. This is what Love reads like, too.

****

Can you think of a similar event that you can choose to perceive as a gift of Love?

May 24
"Love must be learned, and learned again; there is no end to it." Katherine Porter

Terry Z

When I came out of the hospital and started the gargantuan journey back from death's door to a functioning human, Terry asked me if I would do her a favour. Would I create an employee handbook for the dental practice as her final contribution to her employer of 25 years before she retired. Since I had worked for several years as a management consultant, this request was in my field of experience; however, it was still not an easy request – especially from a distance – as I did not have the life energy to travel or interview or gather much information on my own. She had to feed me what I needed about the details of the practice from her position as office manager. I created a handbook that she and the owners felt was suitable and useable. When she arrived at my home trudging in with a desktop computer monitor, CPU, and keyboard, I was astounded. She had decided before she asked me to do her the favour that since the office was updating its computer equipment and this desktop and CPU would be trashed, I should have it (since my laptop had died – maybe instead of me?). She had gotten a new keyboard to go with the gift. I am typing this book on this gift of computer equipment right now. This word is also what Love looks like.

****

Can you think of a similar event that you can choose to perceive as a gift of Love?

May 25
"Love yourself, accept yourself, forgive yourself, and be good to yourself, because
without you the rest of us are without a source of many wonderful things."
Leo Buscaglia

Carol-Anne S

Carol-Anne and I have history. She is my birth daughter who I gave up to let other parents bring her up and love her. After she and I reunited, physically met, and shared life information via letter, email and phone calls, she asked me to attend a shamanic long weekend with her. What a huge gift. Of course, I said I would like very much to do this. I was invited to stay at her house with her partner the night before leaving for the wilderness to take in the shamanic weekend entitled, "Death of the Ego." We stayed in our respective tents, and spent a long weekend being reverential in our intention to pay attention to helping our spirits and souls to move from where we had been to a new vibration – a new frequency. This happened a long time ago. It has changed my life forever. This is definitely what Love asks, gives – and feels like.
****

Can you think of a similar event that you can choose to perceive as a gift of Love?

_____

_____

_____

_____

_____

_____

_____

_____

_____

_____

_____

_____

_____

_____

May 26
"When we are doing what we love, we don't care about time. For at least at that moment, time doesn't exist and we are truly free." Marcia Wieder

Les O

When I needed to leave a bad relationship on a moment's notice, Les and his wife offered their garage to store my worldly possessions in temporarily. Les also came on a moment's notice and helped me move during a rain storm taking time off from work. This is what Love does, too.

****

Can you think of a similar event that you can choose to perceive as a gift of Love?

_____

_____

_____

_____

_____

_____

_____

_____

_____

_____

_____

_____

_____

_____

_____

_____

_____

_____

May 27

"The principle of love within us is an attribute of the Deity, and it is placed within us to be dispensed independently according to our own will." Brigham Young

Heidi O

I met Heidi at the farmer's market. She makes the most beautiful jewelry. She has black curly hair, a svelte body, an engaging smile, and an energy that constantly bubbles out of her. She also makes old-fashioned cinnamon rolls that are exquisite. When I was confined to the house and in the wheelchair, she would deliver cinnamon rolls to my house on her way home from the market. Since then, every time I see her we hug. She is in her 20s. I am in my 60s. I can't even pronounce her last name. She is one of these beautiful spirits in a human body. Another colour band of Love.

****

Can you think of a similar event that you can choose to perceive as a gift of Love?

_____

_____

_____

_____

_____

_____

_____

_____

_____

_____

_____

_____

_____

_____

_____

_____

May 28

"Love is a fire. But whether it is going to warm your heart or burn down your house, you can never tell." Joan Crawford

Mommy G

When I was in the hospital in congestive heart failure, all my fluids and sodium intake were carefully monitored. Since the third day's gift of the popsicle from the specialist who had worked tirelessly to save my life, I then had a hankering for a popsicle on occasion. When I asked around the 10th day there if I could have a popsicle, I was denied by the nursing staff as the fluid not being able to be monitored. I told this to Mom when she was in that day. The next day when she came to visit, she brought a plastic bag out of her large purse that had ice wrapped in more plastic bags that then had a paper towel wrapped around a popsicle that she surreptitiously handed me. She had let it melt on a plate, then measured the liquid. It came out to be one-quarter of a cup. Another slurpy taste of Love.

****

Can you think of a similar event that you can choose to perceive as a gift of Love?

May 29
"Love is the beauty of the soul." St. Aurelius Augustine

Sarah G

Sarah has two beautiful children. She has always given me a picture of the two of them in a Christmas card. I treasure these pictures showing her children as they are growing into two beautiful young people. This is what Love looks like.

****

Can you think of a similar event that you can choose to perceive as a gift of Love?

May 30
"Approach love and cooking with reckless abandon." Dalai Lama XIV

Jeannie A

Jeannie invited me for dinner to her home by the sea. I love the sea and was so honoured to be invited. When I got there, she showed me around her absolutely delightful inner sanctuary, the flower gardens, and we did a self-healing qigong session in her living room together. Excellent workout. Then she telephoned her next door neighbour and life-time friend to invite her to join us for dinner. She had everything already prepared and out came a broccoli/raisin salad, a mango/nut mixed salad with quinoa, and chicken breasts went on the grill. Wine was opened. Within no time we were sitting at the table eating and sharing life stories. She had a cherry pie with ice cream for dessert. What a beautiful meal, shared with gentle, laughing women – the best kind of digestive enzymes available. A zesty taste of Love.

****

Can you think of a similar event that you can choose to perceive as a gift of Love?

May 31

"What most people need to learn in life is how to love people and use things instead of using people and loving things." Author Unknown

Philip H

The door bell rang - there was Philip, my next door neighbour. He was perspiring as it was hot and very humid. He had a bag in his hand and offered it to me. In it were yellow beans and a zucchini that he had just picked from his garden. What a wonderful gift. He stepped in and said that a year ago today he had been in hospital having a quadruple heart bypass and that he felt a lot better this year. Tomorrow would be his birthday. He said that he was waiting to have his knee operated on for arthritis and did I know about the bone he and his mother had removed from his leg when he was a young boy. He had told me this before and shown me the hole in his leg. I thanked him for the wonderful gift of vegetables and cooked the beans up right after he left. What a wonderful kind neighbour. This is what Love looks and tastes like.

****

Can you think of a similar event that you can choose to perceive as a gift of Love?

_____

_____

_____

_____

_____

_____

_____

_____

_____

_____

_____

_____

_____

_____

June 1

"If you want others to be happy, practice compassion. If you want to be happy, practice compassion." The Dalai Lama

Dr. Russell G

We all gathered at the seaside in the fog in the late afternoon with all our paraphernalia. One brought the wood and cooking pot and wieners. Another brought vegetables and dip and fruit and dip and hot dog buns and butter and plates and paper towel and drinks and corn and chairs. Another brought corn and more butter and marshmallows and chairs. And what did Russ bring? Lobster! This was not on the menu, but here it was – lobster was to go into the pot after the corn was cooked – and in seawater from the ocean – the perfect ratio of salt to water in which to cook the lobster. What a surprise and treat! Another taste of Love.

****

Can you think of a similar event that you can choose to perceive as a gift of Love?

_____

_____

_____

_____

_____

_____

_____

_____

_____

_____

_____

_____

_____

_____

_____

_____

June 2

"Love is the river of life in the world." Henry Ward Beecher

Daddy G

Dad was not invited nor would he have desired to come to the seaside corn boil/wiener cook-off, but he contributed anyway. He found, gathered, cut, and whittled the ends to a sharp sliver point of many bamboo sticks for us to use to put our marshmallows and wieners on to hold over the open fire pit and cook. They worked beautifully, did not scorch or burn, held the foodstuffs well, and were long enough so that no one got too hot by being too close to the fire to cook the food. Another surprise gift of Love.

****

Can you think of a similar event that you can choose to perceive as a gift of Love?

_____

_____

_____

_____

_____

_____

_____

_____

_____

_____

_____

_____

_____

_____

_____

_____

June 3
"Love distills desire upon the eyes, love brings bewitching grace into the heart."
Euripides

Jane G

When I was looking to detox my body, one of the items to be addressed was my well water. I was looking for an economical way to have my water tested for several heavy metals and I mentioned this to Jane.

I knew I could take a sample to the province's major city; however, this was almost an hour's drive one way from my house. Jane found another water tester that is only 20 minutes from where I live. This, too, is what Love looks like.

****

Can you think of a similar event that you can choose to perceive as a gift of Love?

_____

_____

_____

_____

_____

_____

_____

_____

_____

_____

_____

_____

_____

_____

_____

_____

_____

June 4
"True love doesn't have a happy ending: True love doesn't HAVE an ending."
Author Unknown

Ben K

I had to really think about this event to see the love buried in it. A couple of years ago a thought crossed my mind that I should go on Facebook and see if a previous lover was there. I did. He was. I sent an email and asked how he was. He answered that I must have heard he was separated. I said no, I had not. We shared emails back and forth for a short time. During one of these emails, he sent me the following poem.

Drove by your house ,"Your parents house"
Just past the tracks that used to be
Do that once in a while.
Up Pelton Mountain, last fall,
I remember fondly things that were and smile.
your family was there, BBQ
they were on the deck, it looked
good to me. I wanted to stop.
Old memories they haunt me, love them all.

Whether it is new love or old love, Love still finds its way into the recesses of our DNA and reaffirms our soul source memory.

****

Can you think of a similar event that you can choose to perceive as a gift of Love?

_____

_____

_____

_____

_____

_____

_____

_____

_____

_____

_____

June 5

"Only love can penetrate all your karmas and resistances and set your heart on fire with the awareness of its true nature." Gurumayi Chidvilasananda

Ella F

After my shattered leg experience when I was starting to relearn how to walk and put weight on a damaged limb, I really wanted my flower garden and strawberry patch weeded. I was whining, as I am sometimes wont to do, to my life-time friend, Ella. She offered to come and weed. What a huge gift. She came and weeded and weeded and weeded for a couple of days. This would be totally back-breaking exercise for me. She did it on her hands and knees. Love grew in the strawberries and the flowers that she saved from the weeds. She is older than I. I am so grateful.

****

Can you think of a similar event that you can choose to perceive as a gift of Love?

June 6

"Come live in my heart, and pay no rent." Samuel Lover

Melvin D

I didn't get up very early that Monday. Too much laughing on the weekend tired me out. When I did get up and was getting ready to take a hamper of clean wet clothes out to the stoop to hang on the line to dry, I noticed a cup of coffee with sugar and cream separate on the little chair on the landing. What a gift. I wondered, now, who could this gift be from? I thought about it for awhile and then decided to let the wondering go. I would be enlightened when the timing was right. I got on with my morning (at least what was left of it after sleeping in!) and about 1:30 in the afternoon the phone rang. I answered to find Melvin on the end of the line. He said he had been in, had left the coffee, did I get it?, took some more items that he had stored in the loft of the garage and did knock on the door several times, but, no answer. I now know what Love smells like – coffee, in this instance, left by a kind soul named Melvin.

****

Can you think of a similar event that you can choose to perceive as a gift of Love?

_____

_____

_____

_____

_____

_____

_____

_____

_____

_____

_____

_____

_____

_____

_____

_____

June 7

"We can cure physical diseases with medicine, but the only cure for loneliness, despair, and hopelessness is love. There are many in the world who are dying for a piece of bread, but there are many more dying for a little love." Mother Teresa

Jerusha Y

How can I remember all the kindnesses this soul has given me? Today she kneaded and prodded and dug and rubbed and talked and caressed and massaged my body and then she shared home-made fish chowder with me with a home-made Nanaimo bar made by a son to finish the repast. This is not only what Love feels like (even when I have to hold my breath and grit my teeth sometimes before letting go of the pain) but also what it looks like, what it tastes like, what it sounds like, and smells like. How gifted am I.

****

Can you think of a similar event that you can choose to perceive as a gift of Love?

_____

_____

_____

_____

_____

_____

_____

_____

_____

_____

_____

_____

_____

_____

_____

June 8

"Love isn't an emotion or an instinct – it's an art." Mae West

Jeannie A

I saw the SUV come in the driveway but I didn't recognize it. The door bell rang its cheery ring. When I went to see who was there, a smile greeted me. Jeannie was standing there with a bag in her hand. She came in. We hugged like we do. She had remembered that I had told her I had difficulty finding Himalayan salt. She had gone to the store where she knew they carried it, gotten it, and brought it to me. She lives a long distance from my place. Her cheery smile and surprise gift made my day. The taste of Love.

****

Can you think of a similar event that you can choose to perceive as a gift of Love?

_____

_____

_____

_____

_____

_____

_____

_____

_____

_____

_____

_____

_____

_____

_____

_____

_____

June 9

"Love is the emblem of eternity; it confounds all notion of time; effaces all memory of a beginning, all fear of an end." Germaine De Stael

Sue N

Some lessons in love don't seem so at the time and it is only in retrospect that one can see the gem gleaning. Sue and I shared many summers going on road trips, staying away for a week to 10 days at a time. These were mainly shopping trips, sometimes for clothes, sometimes for antiques. I always enjoyed our time together until one day her voice suddenly changed from sweet to hard and brittle, demanding concessions of me that I was unwilling to make.

We didn't take any more trips after this event. It took me a long time to forgive the imperfections I perceived in our relationship and to release my attachment to what was with acceptance. Having this experience allowed me to also realize that Love comes in many different forms; we have to find the true meaning in what sometimes appear to be unloving situations. All experiences are about Love. It is our task to find the Love in the experience.

****

Can you think of a similar event that you can choose to perceive as a gift of Love?

_____

_____

_____

_____

_____

_____

_____

_____

_____

_____

_____

_____

_____

June 10

"We may give without loving, but we cannot love without giving." Bernard Meltzer

Rene K

As Rene came to the door to return the loaned camera batteries, I noticed that the mourning doves had, yet again, made a nest right on top of the eavestrough right beside my house entry. This had never happened before and this was two days in a row that they were working at creating a nest in this most unwelcome place for me and any one else who might come to my place and want to come in the house. I looked at her and said please help me. I cannot have them making this nest here. Rene immediately asked what I wanted her to do and I suggested getting the nest down. I got the three-step ladder and she tried to reach, but she is not as tall as I am and could not see over the lip of the eavestrough. I got a long pole and she pushed the nest around pulling pieces of it onto the landing. The mourning dove flew off. She then suggested that it should be made inhospitable to a bird and asked for some garbage bags. We cut these up and she got up on the ladder, then up on the roof of the cellarway entrance and duct taped the bags to the top of the eavestrough – not an easy action when one is not tall enough to see what you are doing and are standing on a sloping roof. She then asked if I had ever made a hoola-hoop skirt out of newspaper. I had not. I got newspaper and she made the hoola-hoop, got up on the roof again and duct taped a couple of newspaper hoola-hoop skirts to the edge of the roof at the end of the eavestrough. I have a feeling she might have a little height fear, but she never showed it in her actions to help me discourage the doves. I am so thankful to her for immediately taking on the challenge and doing all this right then and there. This is what Love looks like, too.

****

Can you think of a similar event that you can choose to perceive as a gift of Love?

_____

_____

_____

_____

_____

_____

_____

_____

_____

_____

_____

June 11
"My heart is ever at your service." William Shakespeare

Philip H

When I went out to water my deck plants, there was a very large zucchini lying on the chair. I knew instinctively from where and whom it came. I telephoned my next door neighbour and asked if they were the givers of this wonderful gift. They were. Another taste of Love.

****

Can you think of a similar event that you can choose to perceive as a gift of Love?

_____

_____

_____

_____

_____

_____

_____

_____

_____

_____

_____

_____

_____

_____

_____

_____

_____

June 12
"When we love there is no reason why." Vanna Bonta

Heidi G

The day was beautiful. I had been up early putting the recyclables out by the road for pickup. I had checked my emails and had sent some additional information along to like-minded colleagues. A car drove in my driveway. I could not make out who it was. The bell rang. I went to the door and there stood Heidi. She came in and we sat in the kitchen. She said, "This is for you as a thank you for having us over to your place on Sunday." The fun bag had women's legs with coloured stockings and funky shoes on their feet on the outside. Inside was a mug and three containers of loose tea, one lemon grass lavender, one chocolate mint, and one wild mint. Earlier that morning I had thrown out my favourite coffee mug as it had breaks in the pottery. Here was a new one to replace it – all without any effort on my part. We talked about energy healing and got really excited about sharing the information. She had to go on with other errands. I can't remember when she was here last. This is what Love looks like.

****

Can you think of a similar event that you can choose to perceive as a gift of Love?

_____

_____

_____

_____

_____

_____

_____

_____

_____

_____

_____

_____

_____

June 13

"I offer you peace. I offer you love. I offer you friendship. I see your beauty. I hear your need. I feel your feelings. My wisdom flows from the Highest Source. I salute that Source in you. Let us work together for unity and love." Mahatma Gandhi

Daddy G

The spool bed was thrown out behind an old barn. Dad saw it when bringing electrical service for the first time to the four brothers living on the mountain. He asked if he could have the bed which had the top and bottom but no side rails. Knowing that I appreciated antiques, he made a wooden box for it and packaged it for travelling. He then took it to the train station and paid to have it shipped four provinces and 1200 miles away to me. I had it refurbished and kept it throughout the 40 years I have had it. I didn't always use it, but in the last 15 years, it has been my constant companion at night. After shattering my leg and having to spend considerable time in the bed, having the top spool railing to help me turn over by hanging on to it, has been absolutely essential to my well-being. Dad could never have known all those years ago how much this gift has continued to keep on giving – every night. Another kind of Love.

****

Can you think of a similar event that you can choose to perceive as a gift of Love?

_____

_____

_____

_____

_____

_____

_____

_____

_____

_____

_____

_____

_____

_____

June 14
"We are born of love; Love is our mother." Rumi

Mary Ellen G

Every year I get a picture of the girls in a Christmas card. They are such beautiful girls with such different personalities. I am so grateful that Mary Ellen shares these updates with me. I keep them in my Love album.

****

Can you think of a similar event that you can choose to perceive as a gift of Love?

_____

_____

_____

_____

_____

_____

_____

_____

_____

_____

_____

_____

_____

_____

_____

_____

June 15

"The choice between love and fear is made every moment in our hearts and minds. That is where the peace process begins. Without peace within, peace in the world is an empty wish. Like love, peace is extended. It cannot be brought from the world to the heart. It must be brought from each heart to another, and thus to all mankind."
Paul Ferrini

Karen N and Karen W

After leaving the hospital where my life was saved from untreated Graves' Disease-induced congestive heart failure, and all the body damage that was done, I then was scheduled to go to the City's oncology centre three weeks later to drink a radioactive concoction to kill my out-of-control thyroid. I was, by then, emailing friends who lived in the City what was happening with me. Karen said she wanted to come to the hospital and sit with me while I waited for the procedure. Since I had no knowledge or understanding of what was involved, I felt all the support I could get would be great. She came, met the other significant Karen in my life, and we sat and talked. Both Karens' birthdays are on the same day of the same month. They took an instant liking to each other. How could I not feel basked in love as I sat between these to Karens as we all learned about the RAI[131] procedure to stop my thyroid from killing me. I sat between these two Karens in a blessed cradle of Love.

****

Can you think of a similar event that you can choose to perceive as a gift of Love?

_____

_____

_____

_____

_____

_____

_____

_____

_____

_____

_____

_____

June 16
"Wishing to be friends is quick work, but friendship is a slow ripening fruit." Aristotle

Ken S and Karen W

When I got home there was a message on the telephone answering machine. As it started, I could hear someone clearing his/her throat. Then, two voices joined together and sang "Happy Birthday" to me. They had a song in their hearts and they shared it with me for my benefit. This is what Love sounds like, too.

****

Can you think of a similar event that you can choose to perceive as a gift of Love?

_____

_____

_____

_____

_____

_____

_____

_____

_____

_____

_____

_____

_____

_____

_____

_____

_____

_____

June 17
"Love makes your soul crawl out from its hiding place." Zora Neale Hurston

John D

When I answered the phone just after New Year's, I responded with a Happy New Year. John said thank you but he thought it might not be. He was phoning to tell me that his loving wife, Rose Valerie of 63 years had just passed away that day and the funeral would be tomorrow. Since we live 1500 miles apart, there was no opportunity for me to go to support him and his three sons on this new journey. His being able to call and tell me the details of Val's three days in hospital and final demise and the arrangements to have her cremains used in a rose garden was another act on his part of Love in letting me know. A big effort on his part at his tender age of 90 to call me and share his grief with me. I love him for this.

****

Can you think of a similar event that you can choose to perceive as a gift of Love?

_____

_____

_____

_____

_____

_____

_____

_____

_____

_____

_____

_____

_____

_____

_____

June 18
"Love in its essence is spiritual fire." Lucius Annaeus Seneca

Jerusha Y

After the wonderful creamed rice with raisins and nuts, special juice, and coffee made by her husband, Al, I then went on the table for an osteopath treatment to help my struggling body keep its new alignments and attitudes. When the session was over, Jerusha asked me if I were wearing socks. Since it was December, I said yes. She then got my socks and put them on my feet, knowing that I struggle with this bend and pull manoeuver. Another act of Love, thank you!

****

Can you think of a similar event that you can choose to perceive as a gift of Love?

_____

_____

_____

_____

_____

_____

_____

_____

_____

_____

_____

_____

_____

_____

_____

_____

_____

_____

June 19

"People, even more than things, have to be restored, renewed, revived, reclaimed, and redeemed; never throw out anyone." Audrey Hepburn

Melissa M

During a general meandering discussion at the monthly salon meeting, Melissa and I talked about a new-to-me concept of the ecology diet. Melissa said she had the book. I am not surprised since she is an avid reader and a very knowledgeable nutritionist. She said she would loan it to me. I was pleased to hear this as my friend was coming for the weekend and she has struggles with gluten sensitivity. True to her word, Melissa arrived on Friday before Karen did, with her book to loan and share. Someone who follows through and does what she says she will do is becoming a rarer person to encounter. This is what Love looks like, too.

****

Can you think of a similar event that you can choose to perceive as a gift of Love?

June 20
"In this life we cannot do great things. We can only do small things with great love."
Mother Teresa

Richard G and Shawn G

I was at the computer and saw the white van come in my driveway. As I got to the door, there was Richard and Shawn asking me to open the basement door. They had brought a small trailer load's worth of dry cut and split wood to augment the cord of wet wood I had gotten the week before. Since it was December, the wet wood needs all the help it can get to dry enough to burn and give off any heat, thereby saving the use of burning oil. I had not asked for this gift; however, it was surely appreciated. This is also what Love looks like.

****

Can you think of a similar event that you can choose to perceive as a gift of Love?

_____

_____

_____

_____

_____

_____

_____

_____

_____

_____

_____

_____

_____

_____

_____

_____

June 21
"Do you love your Creator? Love your fellow-beings first."
Muhammad [Islam founder 570 A.D.- 632]

Heidi O

Getting my weekly 'fix' of cinnamon rolls from the farmer's market and from my favourite vendor (plus a hug, of course!), Heidi offered me a smoothie that she had started creating in her booth as well as the rolls and jewellry. This was my first—ever—smoothie, and was it good! What a huge meal one of these is! The taste of Love in that container was exquisite.
****

Can you think of a similar event that you can choose to perceive as a gift of Love?

June 22

"I don't forgive people because I'm weak, I forgive them because I am strong enough to know people make mistakes." Marilyn Monroe

Ian W

Within the first year of what I call my second time around or new life, I was at the local farmers' market when I met a colleague from many years ago, Ian and his lovely wife, Nancy. He was now retired as I was, and he said he kept busy doing odd jobs to keep him active and mainly outside. Since I needed help with some outside jobs, I asked if he would be willing to help me. He said yes and he has been helping me for the last several years. As he told me one day, "I'm a nice man!" He is and I am so grateful he has continued to help me pruning bushes and hauling the debris away, insulating the basement, picking the apples off the tree, getting a load of wood brought to my place, and on it goes. I am so grateful the Universe put him in my path that day at the market. Love comes and stands right in front of us, sometimes. We need to see it and realize the gift.

****

Can you think of a similar event that you can choose to perceive as a gift of Love?

_____

_____

_____

_____

_____

_____

_____

_____

_____

_____

_____

_____

_____

_____

June 23

"The greatest thing you'll ever learn is to love and be loved, just to love and be loved."
Eden Ahbez

Dr. Downey G

When an uncle of mine asked if I could use the computer to find out what happened to three half-sisters of his, I found myself falling into a worm hole of unknown proportions. That worm hole, sometimes also known as a honey hole, is called genealogy.

When I mentioned this to another uncle, Dr. Downey, he offered to loan me his genealogy materials that he had been working on for over 40 years. These included an actual genealogy program with all of his work on Dad's side of the family catalogued. What a treasure trove! I, then, researched the original question about what had happened to the three half-sisters, and started adding material on my other family line in to the genealogy program that my uncle had loaned me of which I had made a copy. His loan has saved me hundreds of hours of labour-intensive creating of family lines and trees. I look on this as another act of Love.

****

Can you think of a similar event that you can choose to perceive as a gift of Love?

_____

_____

_____

_____

_____

_____

_____

_____

_____

_____

_____

_____

_____

June 24

"We are all born for love. It is the principle of existence, and its only end."
Benjamin Disraeli

Kenny S

Kenny is the partner of a very special friend. Some years ago he unfortunately contracted a viral heart ailment that has left him with a very damaged heart, an implanted defibrillator, and limited strength and energy. He is young. He has great skills and knowledge about carpentry. When he saw the 2-inch gap between two tongue-and-groove floor boards in my kitchen one day, it obviously made an impression on him. Some months later he arrived with the specific tools to fix this. He got down on his hands and knees on my kitchen floor and pulled the wayward board back into place and nailed it there. It took some physical effort to do this in a hardwood floor that was already laid and completed. This, too, is what Love looks like.

****

Can you think of a similar event that you can choose to perceive as a gift of Love?

_____

_____

_____

_____

_____

_____

_____

_____

_____

_____

_____

_____

_____

_____

June 25

"It is only with the heart that one can see rightly; what is essential is invisible to the eye." Antoine de Saint-Exupery

Peter and Jackie R

When I separated from my husband, I went into an anxiety-ridden few months that I would never have thought possible beforehand. I had regular panic attacks, couldn't breathe, thought of jumping off the 23rd floor balcony of my high-rise apartment, and was generally a mess. At that time, I had a couple of friends who lived 75 minutes away from me who played and sang folk songs around the area.

One night I was having a particularly scary time and I phoned Jackie. She said she and Peter would be right up – if I could hold on for the 75 minutes it would take them to drive. I held on as best as I could counting the minutes. When they got there all they did was sit on the couch, one on either side of me, and held me. We didn't talk, we just sat with me in the middle being held in their safe embraces. I was and am so grateful for their physical act of showing me unconditional Love.

****

Can you think of a similar event that you can choose to perceive as a gift of Love?

_____

_____

_____

_____

_____

_____

_____

_____

_____

_____

_____

_____

June 26
"Take away love, and our earth is a tomb." Robert Browning

Dr. Emerson S

This might surprise you that I include this in my choice of what love looks like; however, when a friend takes a friend of yours and her daughter into his house, sight unseen, and gives them shelter and food and information, not for one night, but for three days and nights, then this, too, is what Love acts like. This is what Emerson did when my friend, Gini, and her daughter, Lisa, wanted to go hiking in the Canadian Rockies, but did not know the area well before they got there. Emerson has hiked the Rockies and has written books on particular hiking trails and their history. When I asked if he would share his information with Gini and Lisa, he suggested they come to his house and he would do so. When they got there, they stayed there for 3 days. This is what Love acts like.

****

Can you think of a similar event that you can choose to perceive as a gift of Love?

_____

_____

_____

_____

_____

_____

_____

_____

_____

_____

_____

_____

_____

_____

_____

_____

June 27

"Someday, after mastering the winds, the waves, the tides and gravity, we shall harness for God the energies of love, and then, for a second time in the history of the world, man will have discovered fire." Pierre Teilhard de Chardin

Ella F

I live in a draughty 70+ year old house. When I was in bed with my shattered leg, my lifetime friend, Ella, came to visit. Since it was Winter, the draughts were very noticeable. The Fall before the fall that shattered my leg, I had gotten some heavy-duty plastic and double-sided tape with the intent to seal up the outside door in my bedroom and the outside window in my bedroom's powder room. I had not done it before being disabled. Ella said she could and would do it for me. She got the 3-step ladder, the tape, the plastic, and cutting tools and spent some considerable time sealing the air leaks around my bedroom outside door and closing the air leaks from the powder room's window. What a difference this action of love made to my comfort that Winter. Another hue of Love.

****

Can you think of a similar event that you can choose to perceive as a gift of Love?

_____

_____

_____

_____

_____

_____

_____

_____

_____

_____

_____

_____

_____

_____

June 28

"Love is the enchanted dawn of every heart." Lamartine

Janos N

I rented part of the upstairs to Janos to practice his massage therapy business. After a couple of weeks, he offered to give me an energy alignment massage as he noticed I was favouring one side when I was walking. I accepted.

I thought this was a huge gift, both him noticing an imbalance in my gait and his offering a free session with him. Since I had been seeing only female practitioners, this was the first time I saw a male one. I felt no apprehension and he was completely professional and able to put me at ease immediately. He helped me immensely and I won't forget this offering gesture of Love.

****

Can you think of a similar event that you can choose to perceive as a gift of Love?

_____

_____

_____

_____

_____

_____

_____

_____

_____

_____

_____

_____

_____

_____

_____

June 29
"All you need is love. But a little chocolate now and then doesn't hurt." Charles Schulz

Toni C

After a couple of years of teaching across the hall from one another and driving back and forth to the City to take additional university classes with Dennis C, I got a call from Toni. She said that I was spending more time with her husband than she was and she would like to meet me. I was invited to Sunday brunch.

What a celebration of life those Sunday brunches came to be! Toni has unbounded energy, attracts intelligent, gifted people to her table to discourse on a variety of topics making conversation always enjoyable and enlightening. She always had fresh flowers on the table, exquisitely set with always someone new at the table with whom to share. We had the full deal – eggs, bacon, mushrooms, tomato, perhaps a little salad, toast, fresh fruit, loads of coffee, and, most important of all, genuine enjoyable sharing over the breaking of bread. This is what Love looks like, tastes like, sounds like, and feels like.

****

Can you think of a similar event that you can choose to perceive as a gift of Love?

_____

_____

_____

_____

_____

_____

_____

_____

_____

_____

_____

_____

_____

June 30

"Perhaps that is what love is: the momentary or prolonged refusal to think of another person in terms of power." Phyllis Rose

Jerusha Y

The phone rang. Jerusha was on the other end. She was missing me. She had a request for me. Did I have the time to listen. She has saved my life. I have the time to listen – always.

She had had a particularly heavy workload for the last couple of days and her body was showing the wear and tear by feeling like it might get either a cold or the flu that was going around. She had done what she could to stay the settling in of an infection and was on her way to visit with Donna T. Donna was having a serious operation in two days' time and there was concern that she might have another stroke during the operation.

"Would I hold Jerusha safely in my heart while she was with Donna so that she would not impart any infections and keep both of them safe?" What do you say when the person who has saved your life asks such a question? I said, "Thank you." I said thank you because being asked to lovingly hold both Jerusha while she was visiting Donna in my heart, and to lovingly hold Donna in my heart for her upcoming operation, was validation of why I did not die and was another reason of why I was still here – to not only get love but to give love whenever and wherever it might do its miraculous mending. They are still being gently held in my heart. This is what Love feels like.

****

Can you think of a similar event that you can choose to perceive as a gift of Love?

_____

_____

_____

_____

_____

_____

_____

_____

_____

_____

_____

_____

July 1
"The first duty of love is to listen." Paul Tillich

Dale G

Dale telephoned to say that Jerusha told her I might like to have a visit of her and Charlie, the little white dog. Of course I would. When would they like to come. Ok, then 2 o'clock it is. Neither of them had been to my place before. While I stoked the wood fire, we talked. In fact, we talked for the better part of 3 hours. What a gift to meet someone new, to hear someone new's orientation and attitudes toward life. What a gift that visit was. This, too, is what Love sounds like.

****

Can you think of a similar event that you can choose to perceive as a gift of Love?

_____

_____

_____

_____

_____

_____

_____

_____

_____

_____

_____

_____

_____

_____

_____

July 2

"Love is much nicer to be in than an automobile accident, a tight girdle, a higher tax bracket or a holding pattern over Philadelphia." Judith Viorst

Karen W

The doorbell rang. I went to see Karen with two boxes of wood – one kindling from her outdoor sauna, slow-burning little pieces of wood, and one of dry chunked hard wood. Since she was here for the weekend and saw that I was attempting to make heat with sap-laden, water-logged wood, she went home and came back with this present. She had to drive 45 minutes to get home and 45 minutes to come back to my place the next day and then go back home again. This feels like the heat of Love to me.

****

Can you think of a similar event that you can choose to perceive as a gift of Love?

_____

_____

_____

_____

_____

_____

_____

_____

_____

_____

_____

_____

_____

_____

July 3

"The one thing we can never get enough of is love. And the one thing we never give enough of is love." Henry Miller

Shifra H

Although Shifre Hendrie of Quantum Healing has never met me, she has made a huge impact on my life by offering spiritual gurus through free webinars. I listened to these when I wasn't able to actively participate in other life events because of health issues. She will never know that I think of these free webinar offerings as an act of Love.

****

Can you think of a similar event that you can choose to perceive as a gift of Love?

_____

_____

_____

_____

_____

_____

_____

_____

_____

_____

_____

_____

_____

_____

_____

_____

_____

July 4

"Listening is an attitude of the heart, a genuine desire to be with another which both attracts and heals." J. Isham

Dr. Paula McM

While hanging on to this life by a thread, Dr. Paula was sitting in the chair of my regular family physician, the keeper of my health records since I had stopped seeing her some years before this crisis. Dr. Paula would come every day and sit beside my hospital bed and hold my hand all the while talking to me without ever taking her eyes off mine.

I know she was doing this to try to hold me here on this plane of existence. I understood this on some level. She did not have to do this. Many times when a person is admitted to hospital and the hospital charge physician takes over care, the family physician never sets foot in the hospital to see the patient. I also know that Dr. Paula's gesture, done regularly over several days, was also a gift of Love.

****

Can you think of a similar event that you can choose to perceive as a gift of Love?

_____

_____

_____

_____

_____

_____

_____

_____

_____

_____

_____

_____

_____

_____

_____

July 5

"Love many things, for therein lies the true strength, and whosoever loves much performs much, and can accomplish much, and what is done in love is done well."
Vincent van Gogh

David C

I was the staff coordinator of the Grade 11 students' creation of the College yearbook for five years in a row. At the end of that time, I saw a conference being offered in Seattle, Washington for a week on Accelerated Learning. Always being the one to attempt to do my job better and not accept the status quo, I asked if I might be considered for funding to attend.

David was the person who could say yes or no to this request. When I asked, he said yes, but not because of what the conference was about. He said yes as a thank you for being the staff coordinator for the yearbook creation for five years in a row – not an easy extra-curricular activity, which he must have totally understood. Attending this conference took me from the Atlantic coast of North America to the Pacific coast, being put up in a hotel for six nights, meals during the day, and attendance at the conference. I met people ahead of their time in the field of learning research and brought some excellent skills back that I shared with other colleagues and used to advantage with students over the course of my teaching career.

David didn't have to fund my request. There were many other colleague requests for valid professional development funding, too. This was a testament to David and I look back on this opportunity as a gift of learning more about Love.

****

Can you think of a similar event that you can choose to perceive as a gift of Love?

_____

_____

_____

_____

_____

_____

_____

_____

_____

_____

_____

July 6
"Once you have learned to love, you will have learned to live." Author Unknown

Richard G

Richard had been in a bad motorcycle accident about 20 years previous where his shoulder caused him pain when working as an electrician "hauling wire" as the saying goes for what electricians need to do to do their work. His rotator cuff was in crisis.

I gave him a gift certificate to see an osteopath/masseuse for treatment instead of having surgery. He did not use the gift for almost a year, when, I guess the pain got bad enough, that he was willing to try anything for relief – obviously, a man thing. Once he finally had one treatment, he has continued ever since and I hear no more about surgery although he still has pain, but not at the level it was. Him getting to the point of thinking about massage and osteopathy as treatments and not fluff took a lot of mental gymnastics, I am sure. His having faith in me enough to try one session, is also what Love looks like.

****

Can you think of a similar event that you can choose to perceive as a gift of Love?

July 7

"I believe that unarmed truth and unconditional love will have the final word in reality.
This is why right, temporarily defeated, is stronger than evil triumphant."
Martin Luther King

Mary R

After Mary and I retired, we would see each other on occasion, either at her house or at mine. We always had very interesting conversations about an assortment of topics.

One time, when I had just dropped in to see her without letting her know I was coming, she insisted on giving me a whole chicken that she had raised on her little micro-farm. It was, of course, butchered and plucked and cleaned and ready to go in the pot. I was stunned at this gesture of generosity and consider it another taste of Love.

****

Can you think of a similar event that you can choose to perceive as a gift of Love?

_____

_____

_____

_____

_____

_____

_____

_____

_____

_____

_____

_____

_____

_____

July 8

"Neither love nor fire can subsist without perpetual motion; both cease to live so soon as they cease to hope, or to fear." Francois VI Duc de La Rochefoucauld

Lella G

When I originally started writing, I really didn't know how to do it. I was ever so tentative and unsure. I mentioned this to Lella who would come and look after my feet when I was unable to bend enough to do it myself because of the fluid retention damage from the life crisis. She offered to contact a friend of hers at the University and have her contact me about giving me some feedback as she taught creative writing. I would never have known about this person and her ability unless Lella had shared this information with me. Love-sharing, that's what this was.

****

Can you think of a similar event that you can choose to perceive as a gift of Love?

_____

_____

_____

_____

_____

_____

_____

_____

_____

_____

_____

_____

_____

_____

July 9

"The important thing is not to think much, but to love much; and so, do that which best stirs you to love." Saint Teresa of Avila

Lee R

Over the more than 20 years that I taught university and college students, I rarely had a sense of whether or not I had ever helped anyone. But…every once in awhile, a student would do something to reinforce my reason for continuing to facilitate learning.

Lee was one of those beautiful people. When we had finished our time together over two courses worth of work, she presented me with, not one, but two, of her original painted pieces of art. They are inscribed on the back from her to me. I treasure these, have them in the living room where I see them every day, never take them for granted, and know they are expressions of Love.

****

Can you think of a similar event that you can choose to perceive as a gift of Love?

_____

_____

_____

_____

_____

_____

_____

_____

_____

_____

_____

_____

_____

_____

July 10

"We are an arrogant species, full of terrible potential, but we also have a great capacity for love, friendship, generosity, kindness, faith, hope, and joy." Dean Koontz

Ferne MacL and Shelley M

After I came out of the hospital the first time, still very much in congestive heart failure, still very clearly not of this world just yet, still very cold, a former colleague came to visit. She said she and another former colleague had been to a conference in the City and had wandered around the waterfront shops. They had gotten a beautiful light-weight wool open poncho-style shawl for me, knowing how cold I was, even though it was June. That shawl has been just the right weight and just the right warmth on many an occasion when I could not get warm. Another hue of what Love feels like.

****

Can you think of a similar event that you can choose to perceive as a gift of Love?

July 11
"Love is most nearly itself when here and now cease to matter." T.S. Eliot

Colleen B-W

Through a friend, I was invited to attend six months' worth of weekly sessions conducted by Colleen on the topic of Love. Colleen graciously accepted me into the little group, even though the workshop had already started. We would have a pot luck lunch of healthy organic dishes and then we would do our "work."

Our "work" consisted of prayers, meditations, group discussions, listening to seminar speakers on any topic related to Love. I look back on these workshop sessions conducted by Colleen and am amazed at her generosity of spirit and ability to put together such a powerful workshop and deliver it with aplomb. Fittingly, the subject of Love was also a gift of Love.

****

Can you think of a similar event that you can choose to perceive as a gift of Love?

_____

_____

_____

_____

_____

_____

_____

_____

_____

_____

_____

_____

_____

_____

_____

July 12
"Love is not to be purchased, and affection has no price." St. Jerome

Daddy G

Coming out of the massage therapist's home, I saw that it was the time of year when the university students divest themselves of their furniture instead of taking it home to far-off countries by putting it by the curb for the Spring cleanup collection. In one pile, I saw a double bed frame without the mattress or the springs, just the wooden frame with a cloth topping. I immediately thought this would make an excellent starter for a raised garden bed, no pun intended, or maybe just a little bit.

However, my little car would not carry this form on its top and definitely not inside of the car, either. I called Daddy G. He owned an older 1/2ton truck; however, because of its age, he babied it along with home repairs to keep it on the road. He was very reticent to loan it out; however, he did.

I drove out to his place, borrowed his truck and with the help of a friend, brought the bed form home and placed it on the lawn where it would become repurposed into a raised garden bed. Daddy G loaning his truck against his better wishes, is also what Love acts like.

****

Can you think of a similar event that you can choose to perceive as a gift of Love?

_____

_____

_____

_____

_____

_____

_____

_____

_____

_____

_____

_____

July 13

"There is always some madness in love. But there is also always some reason in madness." Friedrich Wilhelm Nietzsche

Dr. Tracy E

Even though Tracy lived 3,000 miles from where I lived, when I was in the hospital attempting to stay alive from the near death experience, she flew in and came to visit me in the hospital. When she saw how close to death I really was, she chided me as to why I had not let her know so she could have come sooner.

Her concern and her visit are forever embedded in the Love package I received during that 18-day stay at the hospital in my mind and heart, because they were genuine gifts of what Love feels like. With all my ability to hold up defenses gone, I could finally see and feel the strength of the brightness of Love.

****

Can you think of a similar event that you can choose to perceive as a gift of Love?

_____

_____

_____

_____

_____

_____

_____

_____

_____

_____

_____

_____

_____

_____

July 14

"One can pay back the loan of gold, but one dies forever in debt to those who are kind."
Malayan Proverb

Dr. John L

At one point in the last couple of years, the family physician of my dreams who let me have a say in my own health care (radical thought, I know!), stopped running a personal practice and I was without the support of a physician who I could talk with about my hypothyroid issues and possible remedies.

I had already decided when I left the hospital still in congestive heart failure but alive, that if I continued to live, it was time I stepped up and took responsibility for my life, my body, my health (along with the Divine, of course!). To this end, having no human support for my dead thyroid gland readily at hand, I decided to wait until the Universe offered up another candidate for me with whom I could start another relationship as a member of my 'keeping-me-alive' team. Instead, I went to the Internet. There, I found scads of blogs and websites devoted to hypothyroidism. As I was becoming more attuned to listening to my body's intuitive responses of yes or no to opportunities coming my way, when my body resonated strongly with the writings of Dr. John, I listened. Through his website and supplements, I was able to self-administer thyroid replacement for over a year successfully keeping my body working and my heart in rhythm – quite a feat. Dr. John's research and findings and offerings to the general public were a God-send to me during that time. I attribute his generosity of spirit in making this information freely available a glandular package of Love.

****

Can you think of a similar event that you can choose to perceive as a gift of Love?

_____

_____

_____

_____

_____

_____

_____

_____

_____

_____

_____

July 15
"My night has become a sunny dawn because of you." Ibn Abbad

Dr. Anne Q

As promised by Lella, her friend, Dr. Anne Q offered to read some of my first writings. I sent her an email copy and within a week she contacted me. She then came to my house and sat with me and we discussed intent and direction in my attempted start at writing a fictional book. She was ever so gentle in her offerings to not be critical or to put ideas into my head of how I 'should' or 'should not' write. I am so grateful for her sensitivity. I am so grateful for her ability to see that I needed to redefine my objective. I am so grateful for the amount of time she gave me. I accept all this as an act of Love.

****

Can you think of a similar event that you can choose to perceive as a gift of Love?

_____

_____

_____

_____

_____

_____

_____

_____

_____

_____

_____

_____

_____

_____

July 16

"How do I love thee? Let me count the ways. I love thee to the depth and breadth and height my soul can reach." Elizabeth Barrett Browning

Sami

Tigger had settled in as my cat and although he could not stand being picked up or cuddled, he checked on me, wanted a stroking once in awhile, and was generally content. Then, one November day, I saw another cat, grey and white, long-haired, in the same Maine Coon line as Tigger, wandering around behind the garage. He seemed to be someone's cat and I thought he would find his way back home. But he didn't. From January until the middle of March, he continued to go downhill in health, crying with every step across the frozen snow in the backyard with every paw stroke that broke through the thin crust.

I started leaving food for him in January and by March, I could not stand to see his plight. I made arrangements with the vet and one day when I put out food that he now could not wait until I left before climbing up on the step and gobbling it down, I put a blanket around his thin, matted body and picked him up. He went limp in my arms. He had waited so long. After the vet and staying in my bedroom for 10 days with all his body shaved, having been castrated, having gotten an infection in his incision, having infection in his eyes, he emerged only to immediately challenge Tigger as the alpha cat to the death. Blood flew. It took me the better part of three months to get them to leave each other alone.

Sami loved being a lap cat, lying on my chest, drooling with ecstasy, giving me those love eye blinks. He loved me completely and never waivered in his adoration. Another huge gift of what unconditional Love looks, feels, and sounds like.

****

Can you think of a similar event that you can choose to perceive as a gift of Love?

July 17

"To give pleasure to a single heart by a single kind act is better than a thousand head-bowings in prayer." Saadi [poet c. 1200 AD]

Adoley D and Julie H

Two more gifted people who run webinars collecting the crème de la crème of the spiritual and health experts to share their knowledge and wisdom. I have learned so much from the people they have gotten to be interviewed by them, people like Dr. Bruce Lipton, Gay Hendricks, Larry Dossey, Dan Heir. I didn't know what I needed to know until these presenters offered these interviews up and I realized how much I was craving the information. The Universe's way of sending me Love through people I have never met.

****

Can you think of a similar event that you can choose to perceive as a gift of Love?

_____

_____

_____

_____

_____

_____

_____

_____

_____

_____

_____

_____

_____

_____

July 18

"You come to love not by finding the perfect person, but by learning to see an imperfect person perfectly." Sam Keen

Sylvana C

How can you help someone who so needs resolution and allows you in to their angst by sharing deep hurts? Sylvana shared that she didn't get to say goodbye to her father before he passed and she didn't get to help him in his passing.

Her sharing this wound to her soul deeply touched me because she trusted me with her pain. This, too, is what Love encompasses.

****

Can you think of a similar event that you can choose to perceive as a gift of Love?

_____

_____

_____

_____

_____

_____

_____

_____

_____

_____

_____

_____

_____

_____

_____

July 19

"Only in the state of love will the beautiful, fragrant flower of freedom and supreme bliss unfold its petals and bloom." Ammachi [Her Holiness Sri Mata Amritanandamayi]

J.B. D

When my husband and I were breaking up, he said to me that if I stayed in the little town we lived in, he could not be responsible for his actions. He said that if he saw me walking on the sidewalk, he might aim his car at me and drive over the curb and sidewalk to hurt me, but…if I didn't love him, I must hate him. This is how his mind worked, black and white, with no grey.
In retrospect, I know he told me this for my own safety because he loved me. This, too, is another whisper of Love talking.

****

Can you think of a similar event that you can choose to perceive as a gift of Love?

_____

_____

_____

_____

_____

_____

_____

_____

_____

_____

_____

_____

_____

_____

July 20
"Do all things with love." Og Mandino

Brian B

After my sister tragically lost her husband, she found another love to partner with. When she told me that Brian was retired, a golfer like her, and repaired antique furniture and built new furniture on commission, I stored this information away in my mind.

I doubt that I really fell and broke the arm of the Morris-like chair because Brian could fix it; however, in hanging cleaned drapes, I did fall backward and landed on the arm of the chair that broke.

When I contacted Brian and asked him if he would repair it, he came and got the chair (a two-hour drive one way), took it home and repaired it beautifully, and brought it back. I think of this act of Love every time I either look at the chair or sit in it.

****

Can you think of a similar event that you can choose to perceive as a gift of Love?

July 21

"If you aren't good at loving yourself, you will have a difficult time loving anyone, since you'll resent the time and energy you give another person that you aren't even giving to yourself." Barbara de Angelis

Carol-Anne S

Although having a child out of wedlock was traumatic and life-changing for me, the act of giving birth to Carol-Anne was somehow life-enhancing, even during the labour and after when the social worker came to have me sign the papers to give her up. That was hard, really hard. I didn't want to do this – it felt like giving a part of me away – which, I guess I was. I insisted on seeing and holding her before signing the papers although this was totally against the system's procedures. That birth of another part of me named Carol-Anne was so an act of Love, a gift from the Universe.

****

Can you think of a similar event that you can choose to perceive as a gift of Love?

_____

_____

_____

_____

_____

_____

_____

_____

_____

_____

_____

_____

_____

_____

July 22

"I remember when I used to sit on hospital beds and hold people's hands, people used to be shocked because they'd never seen this before. To me it was quite normal."
Princess of Wales Diana

Daddy G

One day in general conversation, Dad said I had no idea how hard it was when he was a child growing up with two critical and severe parents. I told him I knew exactly how difficult it was. What I didn't say was that I felt I had grown up with two critical severe parents, too. I felt him telling me this about his struggle when he was little was his way of saying he was sorry for how we were brought up. I took this admission as a huge gift of Love.

****

Can you think of a similar event that you can choose to perceive as a gift of Love?

July 23
"Love is the only thing you get more of by giving it away." Tom Wilson

Uncle Lee, Ned, George, Bill

Probably because, as I have been told, I was a difficult child to manage, and probably because the teacher really did hate her life and children in general, I was beaten and kicked out of school at the age of nine in grade 3. I was devastated and hysterical. My Uncle Lee worked at the local general store, was living with us, and drove home every day for lunch. He picked me up and by the time we got home, he had a version of why I was so heart-broken out of me.

He felt this was an injustice and a child could not be thrown out of school at age 9, so, we went and picked up three other uncles who happened to be on the school board and back to the school we went. I was beside myself with fear. I remember my Uncle Ned's hands on my shoulders standing in front of him as the four of them told the teacher in no uncertain terms that she could not kick me out of school, nor could she fail me from grading, and they would fix the broken window that was the cause of this retribution. I know each uncle felt the injustice of the situation, but I also know they stood up for me as an act of Love. Boy, am I grateful for that!

****

Can you think of a similar event that you can choose to perceive as a gift of Love?

_____

_____

_____

_____

_____

_____

_____

_____

_____

_____

_____

_____

_____

_____

July 24
"Forgiveness is the final form of love."   Reinhold Niebuhr

Daniel R

At one point, I answered a personal in the local newspaper. Daniel and I wrote for awhile and then decided to meet. He lived about 6 hours' drive from where I lived at the time. I went to meet him. He was gracious, very interesting and we talked about all sorts of topics over the time I was at his place.

He introduced me to a tea called kombucha and I was really taken with it – especially its purported health benefits. When I was leaving, he gave me the recipe to make kombucha and he gifted me with a kombucha mushroom as a starter. This encounter and this gift is also what Love does.

****

Can you think of a similar event that you can choose to perceive as a gift of Love?

July 25
"I love Mickey Mouse more than any woman I have ever known." Walt Disney

Rocky
After an acquaintance had been and painted out my hallway, she came back the next day to finish up. She brought her dog, Rocky, with her. He was less than one year old at the time, a beautiful black Labrador. I was still shy of my gimpy leg being bumped or jumped on and was a little leery of Rocky around my leg. Rocky seemed to sense that my left leg was compromised. He came and lay beside me, beside my left leg, in the pose of a protector. This was a canine gift of Love that I really appreciated.
****
Can you think of a similar event that you can choose to perceive as a gift of Love?

_____

_____

_____

_____

_____

_____

_____

_____

_____

_____

_____

_____

_____

_____

July 26

"To love our enemy is impossible. The moment we understand our enemy, we feel compassion towards him/her, and he/she is no longer our enemy." Thich Nhat Hanh

Margaret D

At one point in my teaching career, I was sharing space with another colleague. One day, a student who had not attended any of my classes although he was enrolled in the course, came in to my space and started verbally abusing me for not giving him an unearned credit. I was shocked and stunned and frozen on the spot.

Margaret, who I was sharing the space with, happened to come in and hear what was being said by the enraged person. She immediately came and shouted for him to Stop and Get Out. I will never forget this rescue as another cloak of Love.

****

Can you think of a similar event that you can choose to perceive as a gift of Love?

_____

_____

_____

_____

_____

_____

_____

_____

_____

_____

_____

_____

_____

_____

_____

July 27

"Love recognizes no barriers. It jumps hurdles, leaps fences, penetrates walls to arrive at its destination full of hope." Maya Angelou

Marianne G

By the age of 18, I had left a village of 200 mostly related peoples, and moved to a large city where I got work as a secretary in the photography department of a major cancer hospital. The department head was a wonderfully brilliant and kind person who took me under her wing and taught me medical photography as well as medical illustration and darkroom techniques as if I could do anything I was given the opportunity to learn.

At about the third year period of my working there, she told me she wanted to groom me to take over her job as department head when she planned to retire four years' hence. I was astounded at her confidence in my ability to learn and do to her level of competence. Her offer and total confidence in my potential was a supreme gift of Love.

****

Can you think of a similar event that you can choose to perceive as a gift of Love?

July 28
"The ear is the avenue to the heart." Voltaire

Lana I

Although we worked together and retired together, Lana and I did not have a closeness of BFF (best friends forever). After we retired, and I survived my near death experience, she and I did share some times over tea catching up on each other's lives.

I had gotten a lovely little rug with Disney characters on it that I used as a cover over the deep freeze. I did the unthinkable and put it through the washer. One corner frayed and I knew I did not have the skill to fix it properly. Lana hooks rugs and does beautiful creations. I asked her if she might be able to fix the corner and she graciously took the rug and fixed it beautifully. I take this act of kindness as another gift of Love.

****

Can you think of a similar event that you can choose to perceive as a gift of Love?

July 29
"There is no surprise more magical than the surprise of being loved: It is God's finger on man's shoulder." Charles Morgan

Vivien M

Many opportunities to grow and learn have come my way since my health crisis that I am still in awe of each and every one. At one point, through serendipity, I attended an energy healing session. The healer talked about our luminous bodies of light and our power to heal ourselves. At one point, she went around the circle and pointed out unbalanced parts of each of our physical bodies. This was within a year after I shattered my leg and had metal and nuts and bolts installed to allow me to walk again. She did not know this; however, she intuitively zeroed in on my left hip and said that I could correct the perceived shorter left leg by 'thinking' my left leg to be the same length as the right leg.

Had I not had the opportunity to attend this workshop, I would still be wearing lifts in my left shoe and limping and probably feeling inadequate about the perceived weakness. Another healing by Love.

****

Can you think of a similar event that you can choose to perceive as a gift of Love?

_____

_____

_____

_____

_____

_____

_____

_____

_____

_____

_____

_____

_____

_____

_____

July 30

"Love is that splendid triggering of human vitality the supreme activity which nature affords anyone for going out of himself toward someone else." Jose Ortega y Gasset

Cheryl MacD

At one point I was actively dying and in the hospital in Stage IV congestive heart failure along with uncontrolled Graves' Disease (hyperthyroidism). After 16 days in the hospital and it looked like I might live awhile, I was going to be discharged the following day.

My executrix and friend and her partner, Cheryl, came to the hospital every day to visit with me and bring stuff from home to the hospital and vice versa. On the final night in the hospital, vanity raised its ugly head again, and I felt I needed some personal grooming care and I asked Cheryl if she would go to my house and bring me back a 16x magnification mirror and my eyebrow tweezers so that I could pluck the black hairs that had grown on my chin while in the hospital. Of course, Cheryl did this and was very gracious in doing so, saying she completely understood my need.

This act was another example of caring Love where she wanted me to feel as good as I could as I started a new chapter in my life.

****

Can you think of a similar event that you can choose to perceive as a gift of Love?

_____

_____

_____

_____

_____

_____

_____

_____

_____

_____

_____

_____

_____

July 31
"One does not fall "in" or "out" of love. One grows in love." Leo Buscaglia

Ronnie R

Sometimes we gravitate to people who are so unlike ourselves, yet unconsciously we know we need what they have to offer at a particular point in our lives. So it was with Ronnie.

Ronnie was a rebel, not someone who liked to follow the rules. He liked being outdoors and working with mechanical things. He found meeting new people easy and many people took to him immediately. He liked trying new things and experiences and when I chided him once on his behaviours, he said, "Don't you worry about me. I won't make old bones. And, I won't have missed a thing." He died at age 42.

What attracted me to him was his kind spirit and his ability to make me laugh – often times at myself. He didn't take life seriously. He totally enjoyed himself and his life. He had a gift of overlooking others' weaknesses and looking for the good parts to celebrate. This, too, is what Love so looks and acts like.

****

Can you think of a similar event that you can choose to perceive as a gift of Love?

August 1
"People need loving the most when they deserve it the least." John Harrigan

Gerald P

When I left Toronto and moved back home, I had also left a good-paying position and was going to not work and go to university instead. I was having the typical seven-year cycle of life crises at the ages of 28 to 30. This meant that I also needed to be creative when it came to spending money.

Gerald drove an 18-wheel truck on long hauls of several provinces at a time. I asked if he would be coming through Toronto near the time I was giving up my life there and moving back home. We made arrangements that he would keep a portion of his trailer's capacity empty on a return trip with merchandise to bring my worldy possessions with him.

I don't remember where I kept my furniture and things for the couple of months that I was in between living accommodations. Perhaps it was at Gerald's? However that worked out, Gerald came in to downtown Toronto, loaded my 3-bedroom apartment's furniture and brought it home intact and unloaded it. I do not remember him asking for any compensation for this act. This is what Love encompasses, too.

****

Can you think of a similar event that you can choose to perceive as a gift of Love?

_____

_____

_____

_____

_____

_____

_____

_____

_____

_____

_____

August 2
"To love someone means to see him as God intended him." Fyodor Dostoyevsky

Linda H

I know Linda as a bodywork practitioner; however, I have also taken in some workshops with her and her partner. When I was invited to their 20th anniversary, I was so honoured to be included in their celebration. This is another gift of Love.

****

Can you think of a similar event that you can choose to perceive as a gift of Love?

_____

_____

_____

_____

_____

_____

_____

_____

_____

_____

_____

_____

_____

_____

_____

_____

August 3
"I will not play at tug o' war.
I'd rather play at hug o' war,
Where everyone hugs instead of tugs."
Shel Silverstein [writer 1930-1999]

Ferne MacL

Ferne came to be a colleague at work. We fell in to meeting a couple of times a month at the local Chinese restaurant for the smorgasbord. Those meals were so enlightening as they included sharing of family histories and future desires. I treasure these times as another taste, look, and sound of Love.

****

Can you think of a similar event that you can choose to perceive as a gift of Love?

_____

_____

_____

_____

_____

_____

_____

_____

_____

_____

_____

_____

_____

_____

_____

_____

August 4
"I have found the paradox, that if you love until it hurts, there can be no more hurt, only more love." Mother Teresa

Sharon S

One weekend my brother was supposedly studying for this dental exams and his wife and I decided to take a road trip in his precious Barracuda around the Cabot Trail for three days. It rained and it was cold. We had difficulty finding a motel to stay in and had to beg an owner to let us sleep in one of his unheated, unlit cottages. We hiked. We took pictures. We played Crazy 8s and ate Oreos as we also could not find any restaurants open that early in the season. We laughed and sang. What a hilarious weekend, while brother was studying – and watching the hockey playoffs. Another trip with Love.

****

Can you think of a similar event that you can choose to perceive as a gift of Love?

_____

_____

_____

_____

_____

_____

_____

_____

_____

_____

_____

_____

_____

August 5
"Love takes up where knowledge leaves off." Thomas Aquinas

Dennis C

Learning about how to take back power over our own health, Dennis loaned me a book by Dr. Hulda Clark. She advocated using a frequency zapper to kill unwanted internal parasites. I thought this was a great idea although I was not keen on buying the official zapper at its price. Dennis, being an electronic engineer, offered to make me one. Not only did he make me one, he also made one for my mother who was having some issues at the time, too. Although the current was so low as to not be felt while holding the copper rods, this, too, is what Love feels like.

****

Can you think of a similar event that you can choose to perceive as a gift of Love?

August 6
"Love's greatest gift is its ability to make everything it touches sacred."
Barbara de Angelis

LaVerne P

While working very diligently at staying alive in the best possible manner by eating clean unfertilized, non-pesticide foods, I wanted to grow my own ever-bearing strawberries. I asked LaVerne to find me some plants. She did this and then came and planted them taking hours out of her busy schedule. Every year that I share the strawberries with the pheasants and other birds, I know that her planting is also what Love tastes like.

****

Can you think of a similar event that you can choose to perceive as a gift of Love?

_____

_____

_____

_____

_____

_____

_____

_____

_____

_____

_____

_____

_____

_____

_____

_____

August 7
"You don't have to go looking for love when it's where you come from." Werner Erhard

Richard G

When my sister wanted to take a night off to go surprise her new relationship partner on his birthday, my youngest brother offered to come and spend the night with me, looking after my needs. I did not know if he would be able to cope or not. My concerns were calmed when I had to ask him to lift my casted leg off the bed to help me get up to move to the commode to use the bathroom. He had such compassion and gentleness. I would never have known this had I not been in this situation for him to express this ability. When I was back on the bed, my nightdress was bunched up under my back and I hadn't the strength of lift myself to smooth out the wrinkles. I asked if he would help me. He put his hands under my buttocks, took hold of the bottom of my nightdress and gave one great yank. In an instant I was relieved of the uncomfortableness. He stood up and asked if it was better. I smiled that yes it so was. I felt love in every action he performed for my welfare while he was looking after me. I felt totally safe. This is another variety of Love – expressed.

****

Can you think of a similar event that you can choose to perceive as a gift of Love?

_____

_____

_____

_____

_____

_____

_____

_____

_____

_____

_____

_____

_____

_____

August 8

"If you have only one smile in you give it to the people you love." Maya Angelou

Mommy G

Easter weekend was coming. Mom was ill. We didn't realize how ill until a couple of weeks later when she was admitted to hospital in congestive heart failure. What struck me was her desire to make a meal for Easter Sunday asking me if I might be able to come. I told her she didn't have to do this, but she insisted. This is definitely what Love tastes like.

****

Can you think of a similar event that you can choose to perceive as a gift of Love?

_____

_____

_____

_____

_____

_____

_____

_____

_____

_____

_____

_____

_____

_____

_____

_____

August 9

"What does love look like? It has the hands to help others. It has the feet to hasten to the poor and needy. It has eyes to see misery and want. It has the ears to hear the sighs and sorrows of men. That is what love looks like." Saint Augustine

Jane G

When I started seeing a medical doctor who practiced biological medicine, it was suggested that detoxifying my body of a life time of heavy metal buildup would be helped by having a sauna. I was extolling the virtues of this new helper in my life to Jane. She told me she had an infared sauna and I could use it any time I wanted to. This is the heat of Love physically expressed.

****

Can you think of a similar event that you can choose to perceive as a gift of Love?

_____

_____

_____

_____

_____

_____

_____

_____

_____

_____

_____

_____

_____

_____

_____

August 10
"Ultimately love is everything." Scott Peck

Dr. David M

When I was struggling to regain a foothold back here on this earthly plane while lying in the ICU, Dr. David would come every few hours to check on me. He always took my hand (I knew he was taking my pulse at the same time, but it didn't matter), as if he could hold me here so that I would not fade away into that state of non-existence. He would look directly into my eyes as if willing me to stay here, to not leave as my tired psyche and body were wont to do. He, plus so many others, saved my life then. This is the power of Love.

****

Can you think of a similar event that you can choose to perceive as a gift of Love?

_____

_____

_____

_____

_____

_____

_____

_____

_____

_____

_____

_____

_____

_____

_____

August 11

"Constant kindness can accomplish much. As the sun makes ice melt, kindness causes misunderstanding, mistrust, and hostility to evaporate." Albert Schweitzer

Lella G

Lella was helping me by looking after my feet when I could still not bend and hold my position because of all the fluid damage from the near death experience. I mentioned that I was going to look for a couple of wooden chairs for upstairs. Within a week or two, Lella arrives at the door saying she found these two wooden chairs, free, by the side of the road. Would I like them? This only happens when one is listening and is also hearing and these can only occur if there is also Love.

****

Can you think of a similar event that you can choose to perceive as a gift of Love?

_____

_____

_____

_____

_____

_____

_____

_____

_____

_____

_____

_____

_____

_____

_____

August 12

"I know that I can give love for a minute, for half an hour; for a day, for a month, but I can give and I'm very happy to do that and I want to do that." Princess of Wales Diana

Donna R

When I was actively dying, I was very cold. Nothing seemed to be able to warm me up. Donna made me a felted quilt and brought it for me to use wherever I felt it would serve the best. This is what the wrap of woof Love feels like.

****

Can you think of a similar event that you can choose to perceive as a gift of Love?

_____

_____

_____

_____

_____

_____

_____

_____

_____

_____

_____

_____

_____

_____

_____

_____

_____

August 13

"When you cherish others, all your wishes are fulfilled." Lama Thubten Zopa Rinpoche

Kelley D

I met Kelley through a former partner. She has always exhibited the same congenial attitude whenever I see her. I will always remember that no matter when I turn up at her door unannounced, she always has the time to sit at the kitchen table, share a tea, and talk for as long as we need to and get caught up on our lives. Sometimes 10 years has gone by yet Kelly is unfaltering in her kindness and sharing. This, too, is what Love does.

****

Can you think of a similar event that you can choose to perceive as a gift of Love?

_____

_____

_____

_____

_____

_____

_____

_____

_____

_____

_____

_____

_____

_____

_____

_____

August 14

"Friendship is...the sort of love one can imagine between angels." C.S. Lewis

Sheila F

There were so many events as I lay on my living room couch actively dying, or passively letting my life drain out of me, that, in hindsight, I am still awed by their continual expressions of love. Sheila came and cleared old paint cans out of the basement and put them by the roadside for the Spring Cleanup. She then went through my linens taking extra blankets, sheets, towels, and then clothes and distributed them around to the various local care bins. I wouldn't be needing any of these things. She was so kind and compliant and cheery and reverent, and yet sad, in all of her dealings with me throughout that six month period. Love flowed freely in my direction during this time and I felt cuddled by its embrace.

****

Can you think of a similar event that you can choose to perceive as a gift of Love?

_____

_____

_____

_____

_____

_____

_____

_____

_____

_____

_____

_____

_____

_____

August 15

"Perhaps extreme danger strips us of all pretenses, all ambitions, all confusions, focusing us more intensely than we are otherwise ever focused, so that we remember what we otherwise spend most of our lives forgetting: that our nature and purpose is, more than anything else, to love and to make love, to take joy from the beauty of the world, to live with an awareness that the future is not as real a place for any of us as are the present and the past." Dean Koontz

Dr. Jenni M

It may seem such a small thing, but, when you are exasperated by 'the system', finding someone willing to listen to your needs and to actually act to support your needs is a supreme act of Love. Such was Dr. Jenni's willingness to prescribe compounded dessicated thyroid medication for me when it was clear that synthetic thyroid medication was not helping and was, in fact, hurting me.
****

Can you think of a similar event that you can choose to perceive as a gift of Love?

_____

_____

_____

_____

_____

_____

_____

_____

_____

_____

_____

_____

_____

_____

August 16

"We are not the same persons this year as last; nor are those we love. It is a happy chance if we, changing, continue to love a changed person." W. Somerset Maugham

Daddy G

I got a couple of strings of solar lights off the Internet. I had always wanted to make an angel to hang in the spruce tree on the front of my property. Now, the idea came to have an angel made on a form to stand in my back yard so I could constantly see her from my kitchen window when it was dark. This would also not inhibit the spruce tree from growing and moving in any direction it so chose. I asked Dad if he would help me. I made a diagram and he then took my idea and made the form. He then came to my place and dug a hole and put a piece of plumbing pipe in the ground to stand the angel form in so that it could be taken out, if need be, but would also have a more stable base. We then hung the lights together and stood her on her place. She has been lighting up and reminding me of this shared experience for several years now. I have had a need to have physical manifestations of angels around me since my NDE and this is one of them. I look at her and know she was made with some of my Dad's Love.

****

Can you think of a similar event that you can choose to perceive as a gift of Love?

_____

_____

_____

_____

_____

_____

_____

_____

_____

_____

_____

_____

_____

August 17
"Happiness resides not in possessions, and not in gold, happiness dwells in the soul."
Democritus

Dr. Tracy E

When someone confides about the opportunity to change jobs at an executive level, then you know you have achieved a certain level of trust with that person. Dr. Tracy did this with me and I know it was an act of Love on her part that I treasure.

****

Can you think of a similar event that you can choose to perceive as a gift of Love?

August 18
"Love cures people – both the ones who give it and the ones who receive it."
Karl A. Menninger

Terry Z

I would not have been allowed to come home from the hospital with the shattered leg if I had not had help. My only sister stepped up to the plate, probably at the request of my mother, and moved in – even though she was in the throes of training her replacement so she could retire from her position, was selling her house and property almost 2 hours away from my place, and she was seriously involved in a new relationship at the time. She took the door off my bedroom into the kitchen by herself so that the wheelchair would fit through the space. She lifted my casted leg off and on the bed when I got up to the commode. She cleaned my body refuse every time I used the commode. She brought me food. She brought me messages from the computer or telephone from friends and family. She ushered people in to my bedroom to visit with me. She changed my bed, changed my clothes, brought warm water and a face cloth for me to wash with. She put her life on hold, even though it was a very stressful and busy time for her. This is what Love looks, acts, feels, sounds, and tastes like.

****

Can you think of a similar event that you can choose to perceive as a gift of Love?

_____

_____

_____

_____

_____

_____

_____

_____

_____

_____

_____

_____

_____

August 19
"The greatest thing you can ever learn is just to love and be loved in return."
Eben Ahbez

George C

When my long-time friend, George, died in his ninety-first year, it was the first time I had been a witness to such an event. It was so absolutely peaceful. After his last breath, the room filled up with what felt like all the colours of a rainbow and it felt warm. This feeling of warmth and colour lasted almost five minutes. I know in my soul that this was George finding out we are more than human material. He never believed there was anything after physical death. I know he stayed in that room because he was absolutely fascinated and awe-struck at his pleasure to know he now had no limitations. He gave me a great gift, being able to feel pure Love through his passing.

****

Can you think of a similar event that you can choose to perceive as a gift of Love?

_____

_____

_____

_____

_____

_____

_____

_____

_____

_____

_____

_____

_____

_____

_____

_____

August 20

"Love is never lost. If not reciprocated, it will flow back and soften and purify the heart." Washington Irving

Karen W

Karen came to my door with two recently started basil plants, one in each hand. She handed them to me. I planted them in my garden and harvested them all summer for the "nutrient of Karen." Another taste of Love.

****

Can you think of a similar event that you can choose to perceive as a gift of Love?

August 21

"All major religious traditions carry basically the same message, that is love, compassion and forgiveness the important thing is they should be part of our daily lives."
Dalai Lama

LaVerne P

LaVerne has above excellent skills in sewing. When my favourite quilt had frayed border edges, she offered to fix it. I didn't realize what fixing it entailed. She took the original border all the way round the quilt off and put a new piece of material on the old quilt so that one would never know it had been done. Every time I pull this comfort quilt up over me, I have an additional feeling of warmth – that of Love.

****

Can you think of a similar event that you can choose to perceive as a gift of Love?

_____

_____

_____

_____

_____

_____

_____

_____

_____

_____

_____

_____

_____

_____

_____

_____

August 22
"A dog is the only thing on earth that loves you more than he loves himself."
Josh Billings

TC

TC stood for Terry and Chuck, my sister and her husband's names. TC was a cross between a Poodle and a Shih tzu. She was a Mother's Day gift to my mother; however, she soon became my father's best friend. She lived to be 17 years old.

When she arrived, she could sit in a cup – if she would stay still long enough. She nuzzled at my neck, wanting to be as close to a pulse as possible, always licking and wiggling she was so, so happy. She never lost this need to burrow her way into my heart and lap whenever I visited Mom and Dad. She loved unconditionally anyone who would let her. This is definitely what Love feels like.

****

Can you think of a similar event that you can choose to perceive as a gift of Love?

_____

_____

_____

_____

_____

_____

_____

_____

_____

_____

_____

_____

_____

August 23

"Love is but the discovery of ourselves in others, and the delight in the recognition."
Alexander Smith

Lauren M

When I was asked to create the space and the time and the materials and conduct a mandala-colouring and drum-making workshop, I immediately had a rush of the feeling of Love in this request. Being asked to do something for someone else is such a validation of a reason for being.
****

Can you think of a similar event that you can choose to perceive as a gift of Love?

August 24
"Love is beyond description; but not beyond demonstrating." Barry Long

Ronnie R

When I was leaving for an extended trip of Europe, Ronnie offered to drive me to the airport. This was a welcome offer and I took it. He casually asked when I would be getting back. I gave him the particulars for nine weeks later. When I arrived back at the end of the tour, he is standing at the gate waiting to pick me up with this huge grin on his face. What a gracious act of Love. He continued to grin and help me to see the lighter side of life over the next couple of years of our relationship. Another manifestation of Love.

****

Can you think of a similar event that you can choose to perceive as a gift of Love?

_____

_____

_____

_____

_____

_____

_____

_____

_____

_____

_____

_____

_____

_____

_____

_____

August 25

"Friendship... is not something you learn in school. But if you haven't learned the meaning of friendship, you really haven't learned anything." Muhammad Ali

Carol-Anne LoP

When Carol-Anne shared how her mother was suffering with arthritis and it was making her ability to stay mobile limited, I offered to share some information I had collected over the past few years in my search for a more healthy life through nutrition. She said that she would like that. Her being open to allow me to share my recently-acquired knowledge with her was an act of Love gracefully given on her part for which I am so thankful.

****

Can you think of a similar event that you can choose to perceive as a gift of Love?

August 26

"Everything has beauty, but not everyone sees it." Confucius

Mary H

Mary and I met while participating in the Love or Above workshop. She was lovingly pregnant at the time. When International Women's Day came around, our whole group, at the suggestion of our facilitator, put on a day of activities in the town's local community centre. Mary's specialty is palm-reading with which I have always been fascinated. During the day's activities, Mary offered to do a reading for me. She was so skilled at her talent and so in depth in her reading, I was astounded at her feedback. Another cascade of Love flowed over me.

****

Can you think of a similar event that you can choose to perceive as a gift of Love?

_____

_____

_____

_____

_____

_____

_____

_____

_____

_____

_____

_____

_____

_____

_____

_____

_____

August 27

"Power is of two kinds. One is obtained by the fear of punishment and the other by acts of love. Power based on love is a thousand times more effective and permanent than the one derived from fear of punishment." Mahatma Gandhi

Mike McG

Mike and I were colleagues. One time I had a party and invited people from different parts of my life, some family, some friends, some neighbours, some colleagues. After that, I had a flood in the below ground basement level where the bath and office and bedroom were. Trying to get some wet boxes of materials out from under the stairs was causing me a problem. Mike was there visiting at the time and he crawled in to the space and brought out the soggy materials. Mike is a man over 6 feet tall; however, he bent his long shape into a ball and did what I could not. Another act of Love.

****

Can you think of a similar event that you can choose to perceive as a gift of Love?

_____

_____

_____

_____

_____

_____

_____

_____

_____

_____

_____

_____

_____

_____

_____

August 28
"The most I can do for my friend is simply be his friend." Henry David Thoreau

Anne M

On my trip less than a year from my near death experience taken with a broken wrist in a cast by train across the country for 30 days, my last stop was to reacquaint with a colleague from over twenty years ago who had also been a friend. I stayed three days with her before getting back on the train and finally coming home. Anne was a perfect host, making me meals, allowing me lots of time during the day to recoup my energy, because unknown to me I had slipped back into atrial fibrillation with the congestive heart failure and was getting weaker from my heart's struggle to keep me energized. She had her daughter and her family come to visit. She drove me around the city from place to place. She took me to her favourite décor shop to meet her friends who she traveled with in the wintertime. We talked and got caught up on what had been happening in our lives over the intervening years. Anne treated me like royalty. Love has so many guises. I love her for this.

****

Can you think of a similar event that you can choose to perceive as a gift of Love?

_____

_____

_____

_____

_____

_____

_____

_____

_____

_____

_____

_____

_____

August 29

"We're meant to live vibrant, healthy lives, filled with love and joy. Of all the emotions, love is the most pure and has the highest vibration." Dr. Bradley Nelson

Fritz H

During a summer of touring Europe with a busload of students of which I was one at the time, the bus driver from Austria only spoke German. Having taken German in high school, I looked on this as an excellent opportunity to learn some of the language from an authentic practitioner. I had a dictionary with me that showed phrases and I tried my limited abilities. Fritz was very patient whenever we were not on the road travelling and would even use the phrase book to choose some of the language challenges for me to respond to when he spoke them. When his wife, who was from Czechoslovakia, and a school teacher, joined the tour, she could speak English; however, she, too, would only speak German so that I might have more practice. After I got home, I also got several letters, all in German, from them, that took me a very long time to translate and then retranslate English back in to German in order to respond. I look on this exercise as another example of what Love sounds and looks like.

****

Can you think of a similar event that you can choose to perceive as a gift of Love?

August 30

"It's often just enough to be with someone. I don't need to touch them. Not even talk. A feeling passes between you both. You're not alone." Marilyn Monroe

Brenda D

After my near death experience, at the third year anniversary, I started saying I was three, three and one-half, four, five years old because this is how I really felt – and still do. On an actual chronological birthday, a beautiful bouquet of flowers was delivered. It was from Brenda. What a beautiful surprise that made my heart sing with so much joy. They were what Love looks like.
****

Can you think of a similar event that you can choose to perceive as a gift of Love?

_____

_____

_____

_____

_____

_____

_____

_____

_____

_____

_____

_____

_____

August 31

"Respect is what we owe; love, what we give." Philip James Bailey

Peter and Jackie R

The more I reflect on events in my life, the more I see the true meaning of experiences that I really did not have any idea how to comprehend their significance when they happened. One of these experiences happened after my husband and I separated and I had moved cities and was on the 23rd floor of a high-rise apartment building.

I would have these full-blown panic/anxiety attacks and I would phone friends for help. One evening Peter and Jackie came to help me. Jackie said she wanted to offer me something that might give me some comfort and help. She said she and Peter had discussed this and she was ok with Peter being my lover to help me at this scary time in my life. I was stunned. I thought about this offer and replied that I was over-whelmed with their generosity; however, I felt this would change our relationship and I wasn't sure I could be ok with the change, so I was declining their offer. The more I think about this offer, the more I realize this was a huge act of Love on their part. It is the only way I can look at this event in my life – as an unbelievable offer of Love.

****

Can you think of a similar event that you can choose to perceive as a gift of Love?

_____

_____

_____

_____

_____

_____

_____

_____

_____

_____

_____

_____

_____

September 1

"Sometimes it's a form of love just to talk to somebody that you have nothing in common with and still be fascinated by their presence." David Byrne

Jon C

When I signed up for the Ph.D. program in metaphysics, I needed several letters of reference. Jon was kind enough to write one for me and although he did not share a copy with me, he took the time and effort to present my 'good side' to the professionals to assist my application to enter the program. This, too, is what Love includes.

****

Can you think of a similar event that you can choose to perceive as a gift of Love?

_____

_____

_____

_____

_____

_____

_____

_____

_____

_____

_____

_____

_____

_____

_____

_____

_____

September 2

*"Grown men can learn from very little children for the hearts of little children are pure.
Therefore, the Great Spirit may show to them many things which older people miss."*
Black Elk

Eliz C

After I had decided to leave my position in Toronto, had sent my possessions on their way back home on the back of Gerald's truck, I still had about a week before the end of my working career in Toronto, and actually leaving to drive back to Nova Scotia. Eliz, a colleague, offered her couch for me to sleep on and her apartment as a deposit for my immediate possessions until I left. The night before I was leaving, she presented me with the most beautiful large pottery bean crock pot with lid. I still have this precious gift and it has only ever been used in which to make old-fashioned baked beans. When they are cooking, the smell is the smell of Love.

****

Can you think of a similar event that you can choose to perceive as a gift of Love?

_____

_____

_____

_____

_____

_____

_____

_____

_____

_____

_____

_____

_____

September 3

"You will find as you look back upon your life that the moments when you have truly lived are the moments when you have done things in the spirit of love."
Henry Drummond

Sheila F
Valentine's Day was blustery and cold and dreary. I chose to stay in and not venture out on the roads or to visit others. About five o'clock the phone rang. When I answered it was Sheila calling to update me on her partner's family crisis and to wish me a happy Valentine's Day. That call with that voice is the sound of Love.

****

Can you think of a similar event that you can choose to perceive as a gift of Love?

_____

_____

_____

_____

_____

_____

_____

_____

_____

_____

_____

_____

_____

_____

September 4

"Let us be grateful to people who make us happy, they are the charming gardeners who make our souls blossom." Marcel Proust

Mommy G

How do you know when someone is really listening to you talk about your present issues? Let me share an example. One Christmas I mentioned that I would like to take Mom's weekly newspapers to use as a fire-starter for the fireplace insert that I use for a heat source. I casually mentioned in passing that the best fire-starter really is the lint from a clothes dryer. Three months later on my birthday, I got a medium-sized box that said a brand of tea on it. Inside there was a plastic bag filled with clothes dryer lint that Mom had saved and gave me. This is when you know someone is really listening to you. This is another example of what Love sounds and looks like, too.

****

Can you think of a similar event that you can choose to perceive as a gift of Love?

_____

_____

_____

_____

_____

_____

_____

_____

_____

_____

_____

_____

_____

September 5

"We've got this gift of love, but love is like a precious plant. You can't just accept it and leave it in the cupboard or just think it's going to get on by itself. You've got to keep watering it. You've got to really look after it and nurture it." John Lennon

Daddy G

I was probably no older than three when I have a memory of being awoken up in the middle of the night and told to come down stairs right away. It was winter and our little four-room house, heated only by the wood stove in the kitchen, did not put enough heat out to warm the upstairs bedrooms. It was cold, so I hurried down the stairs. We had no electrical lighting and the kerosene lamp made magical shapes in the shadows. I remember the stairs were steep with a turn three steps from the bottom into the kitchen. When I got there, a man was standing there grinning with a bushy, large, red beard. He grabbed me up and nuzzled his beard into my neck and face. Mom was saying, "Here you are, your Dad missed us so much that he didn't work out his contract, but came home early. Isn't that great?" All I really remember about this event in my life was the feeling of knowing that I was fiercely Loved. Can't beat that feeling!

****

Can you think of a similar event that you can choose to perceive as a gift of Love?

_____

_____

_____

_____

_____

_____

_____

_____

_____

_____

_____

_____

_____

_____

September 6
"Love and compassion are necessities, not luxuries. Without them humanity cannot survive." Dalai Lama

Karen W

I went to visit with Karen to see how she was doing as she had been challenged for the last five years. We sat on the porch couch and looked out at the wondrous varieties of nature's plentiful baskets of growth. I went to commiserate, console, support, reaffirm her strength for her present struggles with her very core identity. What I got was a most beautiful brunch in the early afternoon that she had prepared before I got there so that all she had to do to serve was finish her masterpiece. She had whipped eggs from their own chickens ready to be made into an omelet. To this she added red, green and orange diced pepper. She had taken hamburger buns, frozen them, sliced them into four thin slices, then toasted them and buttered them – much better than regular toast. She had romaine lettuce chopped up in a bowl. She had cooked bacon and drained it and crumbled it into a separate bowl. When we got to the table, there was the beautifully-coloured omelet, the wonderfully-smelling rounds of toast, the greenery of the salad with a separate tray of handmade salad dressing, grated cheese to sprinkle on top, and the bacon bits. Coffee, wine, water, tea. This is what Love looks, smells, and tastes like.

****

Can you think of a similar event that you can choose to perceive as a gift of Love?

_____

_____

_____

_____

_____

_____

_____

_____

_____

_____

_____

_____

_____

September 7
"Love is all we have, the only way that each can help the other." Euripides

Philip H

When I was dragged down an uneven gravel hill by my car and ended up at the bottom with a shattered left leg, going in and out of consciousness, in one of my conscious periods, my neighbour, Philip, was standing over me saying, "Pat, what are you doing down there?" The nurse who had happened to be there, too, was saying I had to go to the hospital but she didn't know where it was since she wasn't from this area. Philip said he would take me and look after my car getting back to my driveway. When I became conscious again, I was in the front seat of my neighbour's car, sort of sideways with a big lean on toward the driver's side of the car. Philip kept talking to me, but I only heard some of it as I was in and out of consciousness. When we got to the hospital, he said he was going in to Emergency to get a wheelchair. I told him it was way too late for a wheelchair, but to get someone to bring a stretcher or guerney. I don't remember anything else until coming to on the guerney lying in a corridor and my oldest brother, Jamie, was there.

Philip being there at the mail box at the time of my accident and taking me to the hospital, and, which I learned later, phoning my parents about what had happened and where I was, getting his wife to come and drive my car to my home, these are all generous, kind acts of Love, many shades of it.

****

Can you think of a similar event that you can choose to perceive as a gift of Love?

_____

_____

_____

_____

_____

_____

_____

_____

_____

_____

_____

September 8

"If instead of a gem, or even a flower, we should cast the gift of a loving thought into the heart of a friend, that would be giving as the angels give." George MacDonald

Muriel Y

Muriel had never met me when I came out of hospital after surviving the thyroid storm. She had heard of me, but she had never met me. She had heard that since I was so dehydrated from the heavy-duty drugs that were needed to reduce the fluid levels from my chest to my toes, my shoulders and neck bones hurt while resting on the edge of the bathtub when having a relaxing soak. What did she do? She went to a store and bought me a puffy pillow just for the neck and shoulders that attaches to the bathtub with suction cups. I received the gift from her daughter. It worked perfectly. Several years later, it still works perfectly and every time I have a bath, I remember her random act of kindness. Another feel to the power of Love.

****

Can you think of a similar event that you can choose to perceive as a gift of Love?

_____

_____

_____

_____

_____

_____

_____

_____

_____

_____

_____

_____

_____

_____

September 9
"Money can buy you a fine dog, but only love can make him wag his tail."
Kinky Friedman

Olivia Y

At one point in my life, every summer the thing to do was drive to Maine clothing- and gift-shopping. On one of these expensive trips, Olivia and a friend of hers and one of mine went for the week. We laughed, ate, told jokes, spent money, and generally had a great time. Olivia's laughter is infectious as is her smile. When she laughs it includes all of her body. Her father, and my uncle, was like this, too. This is what Love looks and sounds like.

****

Can you think of a similar event that you can choose to perceive as a gift of Love?

_____

_____

_____

_____

_____

_____

_____

_____

_____

_____

_____

_____

_____

_____

September 10

"The subject tonight is Love
And for tomorrow night as well.
As a matter of fact
I know no better topic
For us to discuss
Until we all die!"
Hafiz [Sufi mystic and poet]

Linda B

On one of my weekends off from working in Oklahoma, I flew in to Dallas, Texas, where I was taken in by Linda. She graciously took me around to meet her Mom, her interior decorator-accomplished brother, to her local watering holes with those friends of hers, and even to the grocery store. I laughed so hard when I realized that the grocery store we call and pronounce as the three actual letters, I. G. A., she and they say as one word, just like it looks, only the I is more of an 'ig', then the A. We had a great time visiting. Her graciousness in looking after me felt like a warm sweater of Love.

****

Can you think of a similar event that you can choose to perceive as a gift of Love?

_____

_____

_____

_____

_____

_____

_____

_____

_____

_____

_____

_____

September 11

"Where love rules, there is no will to power; where power predominates, there love is lacking. The one is the shadow of the other." Carl Gustav Jung

Margaret FW

The telephone rang. It was my neighbour across the busy street. Was I home? Was it ok to come and bring some gladiolas? Of course, I said. I had not been south across the road for the last 8 months to visit and Margaret had not been north across the road to visit me, either. She came bearing a most beautiful bunch of gladiolas from her and her son, Harold, to share with me. One was a particularly stunning raspberry red with frilled edges on the petals. We sat in the rocking chairs in the sun room and watched the purple finches and chickadees and house finches and sparrows come to the feeder and flit across to the lilac bush or maple tree to eat their prizes. We visited like is done in the country. What was happening in our lives, what had happened, what was planned to happen. She wasn't here much more than a half of an hour, but her smile, her vitality, her kindnesses, her presence, her 85-years of experience – all exuded Love. I drank it all in.

****

Can you think of a similar event that you can choose to perceive as a gift of Love?

September 12

"A good head and a good heart are always a formidable combination." Nelson Mandela

Dr. Esther C

Not all acts of Love are originally obvious. When the family physician who I got by default would not request the x-rays of my back after the car accident, I took this as a sign that it was time I took back my power and accepted my responsibility for my own life, my own body, and my own health. Although her intention may not have been to contribute to this result, I truly believe that on an energetic level, her higher self was challenging my lower self to remember my ability to heal myself. For this non-action from her human self, I consider this another act of Love from her spiritual self for which I am grateful.

****

Can you think of a similar event that you can choose to perceive as a gift of Love?

September 13

"Happiness cannot be traveled to, owned, earned, worn or consumed. Happiness is the spiritual experience of living every minute with love, grace, and gratitude."
Denis Waitley

Jerusha Y

I came out of the hospital June 8 from my near death experience. The next month, Jerusha invited me to a women's night pot luck at her place. Although, as the saying goes, I looked like death warmed over, I managed to take myself there. It was very tiring even talking or eating during this time; however, the many women there exuded a primal feminine energy that was healing and felt caring to me. Since my protective shell had been cracked open, I felt any nuance of energy shift very deeply. Jerusha insisting that I come and be part of her circle of friends was a huge act of Love that I continue to cherish.

****

Can you think of a similar event that you can choose to perceive as a gift of Love?

_____

_____

_____

_____

_____

_____

_____

_____

_____

_____

_____

_____

_____

_____

September 14

"Tenderness and kindness are not signs of weakness and despair, but manifestations of strength and resolution." Kahlil Gibran

Richard G

I got a call just after I moved in to my present house. It was from Richard. He had bought a 200-year old barn and was taking it down for the wood in it. Would I like the shingles as fire-starter for the fireplace? Of course, I would! He then delivered a pile of 200-year old shingles, the size of which completely filled up one 12x12 foot room in the basement. All these years later, I am still using these shingles to start my fires. Their heat is the heat of Love.

****

Can you think of a similar event that you can choose to perceive as a gift of Love?

September 15

"This is the most profound spiritual truth I know: that even when we're most sure that love can't conquer all, it seems to anyway." Anne Lamott

Lella G

After surviving the Stage IV congestive heart failure life-changing event, it took a long time to regain any level of ability to look after myself in many ways. In a casual conversation at a monthly women's pot luck evening, Lella offered to come to my house and cut my hair. Who does this? Lella does! She followed through with her offer and came and cut my hair. She did a great job following my request to the hair. I look on this act as another gift of Love.

****

Can you think of a similar event that you can choose to perceive as a gift of Love?

_____

_____

_____

_____

_____

_____

_____

_____

_____

_____

_____

_____

_____

_____

_____

_____

September 16
"Of all the creations of the earth and heaven love is the most precious."
Sappho [580 BCE]

Ian W and Mr. P

While out on a drive with a friend, I saw that someone had thrown out a baby's yellow wooden crib. We decided we could repurpose parts of this, so we managed to stuff it in to the backseat of my little car. Never underestimate the power of two women's ingenuity! My friend took one end to use as a gate in her backyard to another's neighbour's backyard. I took the rest and put it in the garage where its future use percolated in my fertile mind. I have always been gifted with creative ideas and one came to use these three pieces as a back drop to a seating area on my property. I had an old, really old, seat from a one- or two-room schoolhouse in my basement that I had dragged home from the beach where it was fulfilling its role as flotsam and jetsam.

Now, I needed someone to make my vision a reality. I called Ian and he came and I explained my idea to him until he could actually see my vision, too. He took the schoolhouse seat home and built it legs. He then brought his father-in-law and the two of them created my vision. It took them the better part of a day, using a ladder, shovel, plumb lines, measuring, digging, cutting, sawing, screwing together, moving patio stones, and whatever else had to be done. It is so beautiful. It is a yellow gift of Love.

****

Can you think of a similar event that you can choose to perceive as a gift of Love?

_____

_____

_____

_____

_____

_____

_____

_____

_____

_____

_____

_____

September 17

"The most powerful symptom of love is a tenderness which becomes at times almost insupportable." Victor Hugo

Dr. Jenni M

It was the first meeting with a new GP. I waited a long time, wandering around, reading pamphlets, completing the questionnaire, wondering how much longer I would wait, getting restless. When the doctor came to get me, she apologized for the long wait. This has never happened before in my life that a doctor would realize my time meant something to me and that I could feel frustrated at a long wait – and actually respond with a recognition to that frustration. Another level of caring Love presented.

****

Can you think of a similar event that you can choose to perceive as a gift of Love?

_____

_____

_____

_____

_____

_____

_____

_____

_____

_____

_____

_____

_____

_____

_____

_____

September 18

"The moment you have in your heart this extraordinary thing called love and feel the depth, the delight, the ecstasy of it, you will discover that for you the world is transformed." Jiddu Krishnamurti

John D

During the last few years of living in Toronto, I joined the company curling team. One of the members befriended me, helping me to learn the game and to also learn other people's names and positions within the corporate structure. His name was John. He was more than 20 years older than I; however, we seemed to hit it off and became friends. Long time friends. Forever friends. After I left Toronto, he wrote me great letters letting me know what was happening with former colleagues and what was happening in his own life. He left the company and went to work for another company in Vancouver. When his house was partially damaged by a mud slide on the hill where he and his wife lived in North Vancouver, he sent me pictures. He was the kindest and 'bestest' male friend to me. Since I met him after separating from my husband, I was shaky and he took care of me. He, too, showed me what unconditional Love looks and feels like.

****

Can you think of a similar event that you can choose to perceive as a gift of Love?

_____

_____

_____

_____

_____

_____

_____

_____

_____

_____

_____

_____

_____

September 19
"Every gift from a friend is a wish for your happiness." Richard Bach

Anna G

Although Anna had moved back to Alberta after her husband's tragic death to be nearer family members, she came East again for the trial where the insurance companies were arguing for and against her husband's estate having future earnings potential decided from his art in progress and art that could have been created had he lived. Anna was so frail and yet so unbelievably strong. When she was allowed, she sat in court day after day after day, listening to arguments being presented by her lawyer and by the other lawyers against her claim.

One day she asked me if I could and would sit with her in court as sometimes the dispassionate presentation of evidence was crushing her soul's resolve. I went and we sat – motionless during the proceedings. I could feel her husband's spirit in the room. I think it gave her strength. I consider her asking me to sit with her a huge gift of Love that she trusted I would have the strength she needed to support her own grief. I thank her for this opportunity.

****

Can you think of a similar event that you can choose to perceive as a gift of Love?

_____

_____

_____

_____

_____

_____

_____

_____

_____

_____

_____

_____

_____

_____

_____

_____

September 20

"Time is too slow for those who wait, too swift for those who fear, too long for those who grieve, too short for those who rejoice, but for those who love, time is eternity."
Henry Van Dyke

Rene K

Rene used to live next door. After the car accident where my back was broken but the GP wouldn't write the lab requisition to have an x-ray, Rene and I would walk early in the morning around 6:30 a.m. She was going through the break up of her 20-year marriage and I would listen to her anguish and she would listen to my ramblings while we walked through rain and snow and went about a mile or two and came back. I staggered along and she took her cell phone in case she needed help to come and rescue us if I could not make it back. I will always remember her for this. I found out many years later she hates to walk for the sake of walking. This is what Love walks like, too.

****

Can you think of a similar event that you can choose to perceive as a gift of Love?

September 21
"You cannot do a kindness too soon, for you never know how soon it will be too late."
Ralph Waldo Emerson

Linda H

I had been without a family physician when Linda suggested I contact a colleague of hers who might be taking on new patients. I did and she was. It took over a year to actually see her for the first time and to become the recipient of her knowledge and kindnesses.

Had Linda not offered her colleague and friend's name and contact information, I might still be wandering around in the darkness, self-medicating – and, although I am getting pretty good at knowing my physical needs, it is still comforting to have a professional on my health team. I view Linda's offering of her friend's name as an act of Love.

****

Can you think of a similar event that you can choose to perceive as a gift of Love?

_____

_____

_____

_____

_____

_____

_____

_____

_____

_____

_____

_____

_____

_____

_____

_____

September 22

"Act as if what you do makes a difference. It does." William James

Don B

After I had been incarcerated in my house for three months, a neighbour who had heard about my plight came to visit one Saturday evening. He stood in the doorway from the porch into the kitchen and talked. I sat in my wheelchair. While he was here, he was glancing out the porch windows toward the northeast where his property and mine intersected with a large tall pine tree. He made the comment that if some of the lower limbs were taken off the pine, I would be able to see all the way out through to Blomidon Mountain. I said yes that was true. We chatted for a little while longer and then he was gone. The next morning, a Sunday, about 9:30 a.m., I heard a noise that took me some moments to figure out what it was. It was a chain saw. Don was cutting the lower limbs off the pine tree so that I could see out to the river and Blomidon. That has continued to be my window on the river and the mountain and I thank Don for this neighbourliness act of Love.

****

Can you think of a similar event that you can choose to perceive as a gift of Love?

_____

_____

_____

_____

_____

_____

_____

_____

_____

_____

_____

_____

_____

September 23
"A compliment is something like a kiss through a veil." Victor Hugo

Cathy T

As the saying goes, people come in to your life, some for a season, all for a reason. I met Cathy when she bought some of my wildflower note cards at a craft fair. We seemed to have things in common, one of them being going for slow drives to see what we could see. We did this often on the weekends and always had a very nice outing.

Cathy introduced to me some of her friends and folded me in to her sphere of activities. How do you know when you are compatible with someone? Your words are safe in their mouth. Her kindnesses were accepted as acts of Love.

****

Can you think of a similar event that you can choose to perceive as a gift of Love?

_____

_____

_____

_____

_____

_____

_____

_____

_____

_____

_____

_____

_____

_____

September 24

"Unconditional love really exists in each of us. It is part of our deep inner being. It is not so much an active emotion as a state of being. It's not 'I love you' for this or that reason, not 'I love you if you love me.' It's love for no reason, love without an object."
Ram Dass

Sue-Ellyn E

Through a casual question from my uncle, I dove in to the addicting netherworld of genealogy. I started with one page of information on my mother's side of the family and then information came fast and furious and I was ecstatic with the amount of connections I found through a myriad of Internet sources. One such source was a sort of blog where people would post a question about some relative and others would reply if they had relevant information.

Sue-Ellyn was one of these people whom I found that had information. And, she had information because she and I are related. Then, I find she is living in the original town where my grandmother's family started. How could I not be interested in meeting her?

I drove to her place, she took me in, sight unseen, fed me, introduced me to her parents, her son, drove me around the town telling me who had lived in the different houses and cottages, filled me with connective stories, bedded me down after filling me up with family history, only to make me a great breakfast the next morning before I went on my way. This whole experience has reminded me of the unlimited number of ways one can experience Love.

****

Can you think of a similar event that you can choose to perceive as a gift of Love?

September 25

"I have looked into your eyes with my eyes. I have put my heart near your heart."
Pope John XXIII

Bob H

When Bob came to pick me up to take me for a coffee at a local café, he noticed the upside down bed spring sitting on my lawn. He asked about it. I told him my intention was to make a raised garden bed; however, at its present height from the ground, it was still too low for me to lean into to garden. He said he would build it up if I had some lumber. I did. He then came another day with his tools and took my lumber and built two rounds of sides up on the wooden bed frame, putting extra supports in along the middles. This took him quite some time and I am so grateful for his gift of physical carpentry skills. My raised garden still produces abundantly every year, thanks to Bob's act of Love.

****

Can you think of a similar event that you can choose to perceive as a gift of Love?

_____

_____

_____

_____

_____

_____

_____

_____

_____

_____

_____

_____

_____

_____

September 26
"There is no limit to the power of loving." John Morton

Wendy T

Another gift. Wendy came in to my life through a friend's suggestion. We share our spiritual experiences and nutritional explorations for better health. We share both having aging mothers who we love and for whom we are concerned. We know there are unseen worlds because we have experienced them.

Wendy comes and brings timely books for me to broaden my thinking, brings rocks for tactile pleasures, even brings Hallowe'en masks found by the roadside that are grand. She has a pixie-like demeanour that is refreshing to witness. She and I share our stories. She is always supporting and caring and engaging. She embodies and projects Love. She can't not do so. It seeps out of her pores.

****

Can you think of a similar event that you can choose to perceive as a gift of Love?

_____

_____

_____

_____

_____

_____

_____

_____

_____

_____

_____

_____

_____

_____

September 27
"Compassion is the keen awareness of the interdependence of all things."
Thomas Merton

Jeanie F

When I started filling in the relatives on Mom's side of our genealogy tree, I reached out to many relatives asking for photos to copy, and names, dates, and places for their immediate family. Jeanie asked me to leave the request with her. I did. Several months later she phoned and asked if she could come by. She came and we visited. She had done a detailed listing of her family and had it all typed up beautifully to give me to add to my growing project. I did not expect such completeness or attention to detail in her response. This, too, is what Love looks like.

****

Can you think of a similar event that you can choose to perceive as a gift of Love?

_____

_____

_____

_____

_____

_____

_____

_____

_____

_____

_____

_____

_____

_____

_____

September 28

"In everyone's life, at some time, our inner fire goes out. It is then burst into flame by an encounter with another human being. We should all be thankful for those people who rekindle the inner spirit." Albert Schweitzer

Harold F

Harold and I share the same birth day. He is my neighbour. Unbidden, he arrives at my door in the Fall with a bag of home-grown sweet red peppers. They are huge. They are delicious. I make sweet pepper jelly. I make sweet pepper relish. I core and slice them and freeze them and eat them all Winter. I think of these succulent gifts as pieces of Love, wouldn't you?

****

Can you think of a similar event that you can choose to perceive as a gift of Love?

_____

_____

_____

_____

_____

_____

_____

_____

_____

_____

_____

_____

_____

September 29
"Out of chaos the future emerges in harmony and beauty." Emma Goldman

Angela P

I met Angela first at Dennis and Toni's Sunday brunch table. Then, many years later, I again met her at Jerusha's women's pot luck evening. Since then, we also are part of a little book club. She has gifted me with the SCBYs [symbiotic culture of bacteria and yeast] that are the starter material to make water kefir. This is such a refreshing drink with so many healthy attributes, I have some in the fridge all the time. Her sharing of some starter SCBYs is also what Love looks like.

****

Can you think of a similar event that you can choose to perceive as a gift of Love?

_____

_____

_____

_____

_____

_____

_____

_____

_____

_____

_____

_____

_____

_____

_____

_____

September 30
"If we could see the miracle of a single flower clearly, our whole life would change."
Buddha

Lenore W

Lenore was Leslen's Mom. When Leslen took me to visit her parents, Lenore and I got on very well. When I got back from my quest months later, there was a package at the Post Office waiting to be picked up. When I got it home and opened it, it was from Lenore. She had made me the most beautiful and whimsical rabbit in cloth about 15 inches tall. The ears were particularly engaging, being extra floppy without stuffing like the rest of the body, where they hung straight down, but could be thrown back to give the impression of flair. Another feel of Love.

****

Can you think of a similar event that you can choose to perceive as a gift of Love?

October 1
"Love is the absence of judgment" Dalai Lama XIV

Scott L

When a friend suggested there was a house that I might be interested in buying instead of renting as I was, I knew my finances were not in good enough shape to even cover the down payment. Since my friend was a real estate agent at the time, she also suggested a particular banker who might be able to help me.

Dad helped me with the down payment and I went to see the banker about a mortgage. Scott did what I call creative accounting that allowed I could afford the house if I rented out the upstairs apartment, which I did.

If I had gone to another banker and not gotten the help Scott gave me, I would not be living where I have been for the last 16 years and loving it. Another gift of Love.

****

Can you think of a similar event that you can choose to perceive as a gift of Love?

_____

_____

_____

_____

_____

_____

_____

_____

_____

_____

_____

_____

_____

October 2
"Life is like an ever-shifting kaleidoscope - a slight change, and all patterns alter."
Sharon Salzberg

Judy K

On a trip to Puerto Rico for a week's vacation, I sat beside a lovely woman from Rochester, New York. Judy and I seemed to have a level of simpatico that we agreed we should correspond, which we did. When she offered a trip to Las Vegas the following year for me, all paid, if I paid the airfare to Rochester, New York, I took it. We had a great week, playing blackjack, going to the dinner theatres, wandering around the shops. I will never forget this out-of-the-blue vacation gift of Love.

****

Can you think of a similar event that you can choose to perceive as a gift of Love?

_____

_____

_____

_____

_____

_____

_____

_____

_____

_____

_____

_____

_____

_____

October 3

"One is loved because one is loved. No reason is needed for loving." Paulo Coelho

Dave C

Would there be a discount for someone who is retired, female, single, physically challenged, perhaps? This is the question I asked Dave after I had chosen the special latex rubber and wool pillow. He grinned and said, "What if we went with the list price without anything else added? What do you think of that?" That was a gift of over $13. I thought that was a wonderful gift and told him so. In fact, I told him that he would be written up in my book on "This Is What Love Looks Like, Too," to which he grinned and thought that was a great addition to his day. So, here he is. This is what Love looks like, too!

****

Can you think of a similar event that you can choose to perceive as a gift of Love?

_____

_____

_____

_____

_____

_____

_____

_____

_____

_____

_____

_____

_____

_____

_____

October 4
"Love isn't something you find. Love is something that finds you." Loretta Young

Karen W

I am still in wonderment at how people come into one's life – at the right time – at the right place – for the right reasons. Karen said she had told no one that she was starting an online program in metaphysical ministry and shared the website information, the philosophy of the creator, and why she was doing this. I said that this sounded like what would make 45 years of my life come together in a cohesive manner that might make sense to me and help me to understand the diversity of my life experiences to date. I signed up. The courses, the topics, the options, the readings, the weekly sermons online, the learnings, were exactly what brought my life together into a cohesive package to this point in time – finally! that direction that I had started on back there in my teens, finally coming to fruition with a doctoral designation. Karen sharing her desires with me – allowing me to travel this part of her path with her – her travelling this part of my path with me - this is what Love looks like.

****

Can you think of a similar event that you can choose to perceive as a gift of Love?

October 5

"When you realize how perfect everything is you will tilt your head back and laugh at the sky." Buddha

Betty-Lou S

Every so often when I was teaching, there would be a special symbiotic relationship that would develop among students in a particular class and me, their facilitator. One such event culminated with Betty-Lou reading the following poem she had penned at the end of a business mathematics course:

"We've come to say a 'Thank you'; From each and every one; For helping us the last few months; And the great job you have done. You added friendship to the math; And multiplied with cheer; Subtracted all our worries; And divided all our fears. And as the new year comes along; We'll think of you each day; And appreciate the formulas; You taught the OAAs. And if we do succeed in life; Or maybe lose our shirts; We'll come to you to borrow cash; Or your $300 skirt. We'd like to honor you today; You are the best, Ms. Dix; You've gained the friendship and respect; Of the OAAs of 96."

How can one not feel Love at hearing this read and seeing the people and Betty-Lou in one's mind's eye remembering all of this?

****

Can you think of a similar event that you can choose to perceive as a gift of Love?

_____

_____

_____

_____

_____

_____

_____

_____

_____

_____

_____

October 6
"Do not think that love in order to be genuine has to be extraordinary. What we need is to love without getting tired. Be faithful in small things because it is in them that your strength lies." Mother Theresa

Helen W

When I took Dad about a two-hour drive to a particular clinic to have surgery on a finger, I stopped where Helen worked. She is a busy lady. She was personnel director to a large plant at this time. I asked at the gate if the security guard would call to see if she might be available for a couple of minutes. He did. She was.

She came out to the car, met my father, chatted for a bit, gave each of us a great big hug, then went back to work, and we went on our way. This is what Love feels like.
****

Can you think of a similar event that you can choose to perceive as a gift of Love?

_____

_____

_____

_____

_____

_____

_____

_____

_____

_____

_____

_____

_____

October 7

"It is the heart, and not the brain,
That to the highest doth attain,
And he who followeth Love's behest
Far excelleth all the rest!"
Henry Wadsworth Longfellow

John B. D

Years after I separated, many years in fact, my father casually wondered one day if John might still be alive and well. I said I did not know but it had been more than 30 years. I thought about this part of my life and thought, hmmm, maybe I can find him on the Internet. I searched several times without success, then I saw his mother's telephone number that I remembered and then her street address, which I also remembered.

I tucked this information away for a couple of months, and then I phoned the number, thinking I would get his mother. No, I got John B. His mother was very elderly and he was staying at the house looking after her. We had a lovely chat and I told him my reason for contacting him. He was very cordial and gracious on the phone. This, too, is what Love sounds like.

****

Can you think of a similar event that you can choose to perceive as a gift of Love?

_____

_____

_____

_____

_____

_____

_____

_____

_____

_____

_____

_____

October 8

"Immature love says: 'I love you because I need you.' Mature love says 'I need you because I love you.'" Erich Fromm

Brian B

On a long driving trip to meet a distant relative, I stopped at Brian and my sister's. Brian was insistent that I should stay the night and go on in the morning. I am so glad that I did. It gave me time to visit and I was refreshed the next morning so that when I arrived at my destination, I could still function for a few more hours before I tired out.

This offer for me to stay overnight at Brian's place, is also what Love sounds like.

****

Can you think of a similar event that you can choose to perceive as a gift of Love?

October 9

"Love is always bestowed as a gift - freely, willingly and without expectation. We don't love to be loved; we love to love." Leo Buscaglia

Robert G

On the front of my fridge is a painting by Robert before he could write letters. They are big bold letters of his name. Whenever I see him, he rushes in to my arms and gives me a great big hug. This is what Love feels like.

****

Can you think of a similar event that you can choose to perceive as a gift of Love?

_____

_____

_____

_____

_____

_____

_____

_____

_____

_____

_____

_____

_____

_____

_____

_____

_____

_____

October 10

"I say to people who care for people who are dying, if you really love that person and want to help them, be with them when their end comes close. Sit with them – you don't even have to talk. You don't have to do anything but really be there with them."
Elisabeth Kubler-Ross

Chuck Z

My sister's husband had a terrible accident where his 44-foot motor home ran over him while he was under it working on the starter. He lived 35 days afterward. About ten days before he died when he was ventilated and could not speak, I was staying with my sister at his hospital bedside when he curled his finger to me to come close. There were tears seeping down the sides of his face from the corners of his swollen eyes. He put a finger in to a tear wetness and put it to my cheek just below my eye. He did this three times, once under each eye and once to my forehead. I knew immediately that he was saying he loved me, my father (who he golfed with and called "Pard" as a form of endearment, short for partner) and my mother, his father-in-law and mother-in-law – and that he was saying good-bye to the three of us with each tear drop, as well. Love gets pretty big sometimes and swells up one's chest like mine did that day. Sometimes, it is very obvious what Love feels and looks like, there's no doubt.

****

Can you think of a similar event that you can choose to perceive as a gift of Love?

_____

_____

_____

_____

_____

_____

_____

_____

_____

_____

_____

_____

_____

October 11
"We waste time looking for the perfect lover, instead of creating the perfect love."
Tom Robbins

Dr. Russell G
Being a dentist, Russell specialized in root canal dentistry. When I needed two molar teeth to have heroic measures to save them, Russell offered to do the root canal work on them both for no cost to me, except to pay my way from my home to his office in another province. This I gladly did. He did excellent work and more than 20 years later, I am still enjoying my chewing ability because of his generosity. This is what Love feels like, too.
****
Can you think of a similar event that you can choose to perceive as a gift of Love?

_____

_____

_____

_____

_____

_____

_____

_____

_____

_____

_____

_____

_____

_____

_____

October 12
"My religion is very simple. My religion is kindness." Dalai Lama

Melvin D

When I was recovering from the congestive heart failure near death experience, my faithful friend, Sheila, was still doing most things for me. One of these helping things was cleaning my house for me every couple of weeks. One day, she offered that her neighbour might be interested in taking over from her as my cleaning person. Sheila's job was getting too busy for her to continue and her neighbour was recently laid off from another job and was starting his own cleaning business. When me met, I knew we would become friends. I never had a male 'house boy' before, and Melvin fit my needs exactly. He was quick, funny, and ever so attentive and kind. This is what Love looks like, too.

****

Can you think of a similar event that you can choose to perceive as a gift of Love?

October 13

"The best remedy for those who are afraid, lonely or unhappy is to go outside, somewhere where they can be quiet, alone with the heavens, nature and God. Because only then does one feel that all is as it should be."
Anne Frank

Gary G

It's not often I get letters from male friends; however, Gary was special. When he and his wife broke up, I offered him a place to stay for a couple of weeks until he figured out what he was going to do next. Months after he left my life and continued on with his own, I received this letter from him thanking me in detail for my kindnesses. He definitely did not have to take the time and effort to write me a letter saying what he had also said in person. This, too, is what Love reads like.

****

Can you think of a similar event that you can choose to perceive as a gift of Love?

_____

_____

_____

_____

_____

_____

_____

_____

_____

_____

_____

_____

_____

_____

October 14

"I've learned that people will forget what you said, people will forget what you did, but people will never forget how you made them feel." Maya Angelou

Henry P

Henry was one of Dad's lifetime friends. He was funny, gentle, and always kind. One day I was visiting him and he showed me his pocket watch collection. They were just jumbled in several shoe boxes. He told me his sons would get them when he died. When I was leaving, he picked out a beautiful gold watch case without the watch contents, and handed it to me. I still have this gift. This, too, is what Love feels like.

****

Can you think of a similar event that you can choose to perceive as a gift of Love?

_____

_____

_____

_____

_____

_____

_____

_____

_____

_____

_____

_____

_____

_____

_____

_____

October 15
"To say "I love you" one must first be able to say the "I."" Ayn Rand

Brenda D
One Christmas, Brenda brought me a multi-part gift. One of the items was a little clear angel. She pushed the button on the bottom and it lit up. Then it started changing colours. When I watched, I realized it was shifting through the seven chakra colours and I thought how lovely. This is a healing angel! Sometimes a gift is even more important than the giver realizes. Another colour of Love.

****

Can you think of a similar event that you can choose to perceive as a gift of Love?

_____

_____

_____

_____

_____

_____

_____

_____

_____

_____

_____

_____

_____

_____

_____

_____

_____

_____

October 16
"What the world really needs is more love and less paper work." Pearl Bailey

Mommy G

You know you have been listened to and heard when you get a call that a cord of wood is being delivered to your house in March when you are almost out of your winter's supply. I had been sharing with Mom in the first part of March how much wood I had burned keeping warm because that winter was particularly blustery and continuously cold day after day. This source of heat is also what Love feels like.

****

Can you think of a similar event that you can choose to perceive as a gift of Love?

_____

_____

_____

_____

_____

_____

_____

_____

_____

_____

_____

_____

_____

_____

_____

299

October 17
"Joy descends gently upon us like the evening dew, and does not patter down like a hailstorm." Jean Paul

Dave T
During the requirement that new teachers spend three summers in residence taking teacher training to continue working at the community college level, Dave plied his trade freely. He gave me a great hair cut, being not only a barber and hairdresser, but also an esthetician where he also helped train the funeral director students as part of his gifts. I still remember the laughs we had over silly stuff when I was sitting while he cut my hair. This, too, is what Love looks like.
****
Can you think of a similar event that you can choose to perceive as a gift of Love?

_____

_____

_____

_____

_____

_____

_____

_____

_____

_____

_____

_____

_____

_____

October 18
"Who, being loved, is poor?" Oscar Wilde

Ian and Nancy W

It was the day before Christmas when the door bell rang. I went and there was Ian with a smile on his face. Ian helps me with yard work such as pruning and creating things I think up but can't put in to reality. I originally met him when we were both teaching and now we are both retired. He likes to keep busy and likes to work outside.

In his hand was a bottle of beets that he and his wife, Nancy, had made together. He was offering them to me as a present. I was overjoyed and so taken with their generosity. Another taste of Love in that bottle.

****

Can you think of a similar event that you can choose to perceive as a gift of Love?

October 19
"Let us always meet each other with a smile, for the smile is the beginning of love."
Mother Teresa

Dennis and Toni C

During that trip to Western Canada to visit long-time friends, I was treated to the most exquisite arrays of flavours. Dennis and Toni had only been in Edmonton for less than a year when I arrived that May with my left arm and wrist in a cast. They took me to the most interesting restaurants. One of these eateries was called Padmanadi, ranked number seven in all of Edmonton. When we walked in to the restaurant where one had to have a reservation, what I saw were old-fashioned booths like restaurants of the 1960s and 1970s. The place was so understatedly unassuming. There was absolutely nothing standing out to promote itself as an opportunity for a gustatory delight. The owner, Korean perhaps? came and sat with us for a bit. The three of them obviously had a relationship as they kept grinning and smiling at each other without actually saying anything. We then got a menu delivered and ordered. The restaurant is actually vegan where all the dishes have meat-sounding names and the food looks like the meat-sounding names; however, it is all vegan. The tastes and appearances of the food were such a surprising experience, that I still marvel at this treat my friends gave me. It wasn't until I was leaving Edmonton and was waiting for the train to start coming back East that I picked up a tourist travel magazine about Edmonton and found the Padmanadi restaurant highlighted as one of the best places in Edmonton to eat. This unpretentious gourmet experience is another gift of what Love looks and tastes like.

****

Can you think of a similar event that you can choose to perceive as a gift of Love?

_____

_____

_____

_____

_____

_____

_____

_____

_____

_____

_____

October 20
"Every moment and every event of every man's life on earth plants something in his soul." Thomas Merton

Ken W

Through my explorations down the wormhole of genealogy, I found a distant relative living in Massachusetts by the name of Ken. He was related through my mother's side of the family. We shared some information back and forth via email since he had information I could not find and I had some up-to-date information he could not find, too.

Then, I received a parcel in the mail of over 80 pages of information he had put together on his side of the genealogy tree. He was sharing all this with me that made it redundant for me to recreate much of the information I was having a hard time locating. This is what Love reads like.

****
Can you think of a similar event that you can choose to perceive as a gift of Love?

_____

_____

_____

_____

_____

_____

_____

_____

_____

_____

_____

_____

_____

_____

October 21
"To love abundantly is to live abundantly, and to love forever is to live forever."
Henry Drummond

Olivia Y
At one point when my cousin, Olivia, lived about one-half hour away from me, I would visit there often. One winter when I was driving on the highway I could see a message on the top of a snow bank in their driveway. It was written in green food colouring in big letters and said, "Hi, Pat." I know that Olivia was the promoter of this sign and I laughed and laughed. Don't eat green snow. Another way to express Love.

****

Can you think of a similar event that you can choose to perceive as a gift of Love?

_____

_____

_____

_____

_____

_____

_____

_____

_____

_____

_____

_____

_____

_____

_____

_____

_____

October 22

"I can live without money, but I cannot live without love." Judy Garland

Brenda D

How Brenda became my main qigong partner is a mystery. That she continues to come regularly during the week after her work to exercise with me is a gift. For Christmas, she gave me the most beautiful little brown pottery pot with its own lid with a little button handle, its own gold-plated spoon, and inside the pot her own home-made, natural, non-toxic toothpaste – coconut oil, salt, baking powder. I use this toothpaste especially after drinking coffee and it works miracles in taking the coffee stain off my teeth. My last dental checkup brought accolades about the wonderful condition of my gums and enamel. I contribute it to my new healthy toothpaste, a gift of Love.

****

Can you think of a similar event that you can choose to perceive as a gift of Love?

October 23

"Since love grows within you, so beauty grows. For love is the beauty of the soul."
Saint Augustine

Sharon M-S

After the car accident where my back was broken and not identified for almost 6 months, I was off work for five of those six months trying to figure out why I was in so much pain. Because of a variety of circumstances, professional help was not forthcoming. When I started back to work, Sharon offered that I only carry two classes for two hours of teaching time per day face to face for the next couple of months and that I continue facilitating other courses via the Internet from home. This allowance made all the difference in my ability to continue working at all and, even through I really should have stopped working then, it made it possible for me to believe I could continue until an appropriate retiring age. Sharon's generous offer is also what Love looks like.

****

Can you think of a similar event that you can choose to perceive as a gift of Love?

_____

_____

_____

_____

_____

_____

_____

_____

_____

_____

_____

_____

_____

_____

October 24

"The beginning of love is to let those we love be perfectly themselves, and not to twist them to fit our own image. Otherwise we love only the reflection of ourselves we find in them." Thomas Merton

Karen W

After taking me to the city's hospital to drink the radioactive thyroid-killing drink, Karen then took me for lunch and then to her home. She wanted to take me down to the river's edge since the tide was in; however, it was too long and too steep a trail for my weak body to endure. She bundled me on the back of her ATV and took me down to the water's edge. It was glorious, wandering along the tidal edge picking up rocks and looking for driftwood with spirit animals in them still. She then brought me back up the hill on the back of the ATV which took all my energy to just hang on. She was very caring and sincere in wanting me to experience new things since I was still such a baby just out of the near death experience. I look on these acts as Love, too.

****

Can you think of a similar event that you can choose to perceive as a gift of Love?

_____

_____

_____

_____

_____

_____

_____

_____

_____

_____

_____

_____

_____

October 25
"Love is the magician that pulls man out of his own hat." Ben Hecht

Doug G

One of the first winters that I heated my house using more wood for heat than oil, I ran out in February. Doug had chunk lumber at his place left over from other projects and he cut all this up and brought it in bins to me for my use. He, then, went to my basement with his hand saw and cut up old left-over pieces of wood from projects here at my place, too. That was a lot of manual labour cutting up that wood. This, too, is the heat of Love.

****

Can you think of a similar event that you can choose to perceive as a gift of Love?

October 26
"One forgives to the degree that one loves." Francois de La Rochefoucauld

Brigit O

Heidi's sister wanted to know if I knew how to sew. Of course I do. She asked me if I would make her a pillow case to carry laundry in to be made out of the most beautiful handmade fabric she had gotten in Africa while there working for international development as part of her university studies. I made the pillow case for her and she gave me a sublime piece of handmade intricately-patterned fabric she had gotten in Burkina Faso in Africa. This piece of fabric to a sewer is like candy to a sugar-addicted child in a candy store. It has yet to be created into a useable item; however, it is just so beautiful – like the giver of this gift. Another feel and colour of Love.

****

Can you think of a similar event that you can choose to perceive as a gift of Love?

_____

_____

_____

_____

_____

_____

_____

_____

_____

_____

_____

_____

_____

_____

_____

October 27
"A hug is like a boomerang - you get it back right away." Bill Keane

Stephen G

When I needed to leave a bad relationship quickly, Stephen came with his half-ton truck and took a load of my furniture to my friend's garage for storage. This was during the day when he had other activities to be doing instead. I remember this action with a feeling of being given a gift of Love.

****

Can you think of a similar event that you can choose to perceive as a gift of Love?

_____

_____

_____

_____

_____

_____

_____

_____

_____

_____

_____

_____

_____

_____

_____

_____

_____

_____

October 28

"To love for the sake of being loved is human, but to love for the sake of loving is angelic." Alphonse de Lamartine

George and Betty C

I moved in to a new duplex one June. That September a Scottish retired couple, George and Betty, moved in the other side. We both rented there for almost ten years. Over that time, they adopted me and I them. They showed me unconditional love. I looked after them until and after they passed on. We had that kind of relationship. Special.

They were gifted in many artistic areas and shared some of their gifts with me. I still have a couple of George's watercolour paintings and Betty's pastel and oil paintings. They invited me to special dinners where they would create new dishes for the first time. They invited me for tea and then they would play duets on the piano. They would recite poetry one line per person with loving smiles on their faces. They would speak in a special Scottish dialect called Doric. I loved them. They loved me. They lived life where every event – even going to the grocery store – was an adventure to be relished in and cherished. This is definitely what Love feels, looks, tastes, smells, sounds like.

****

Can you think of a similar event that you can choose to perceive as a gift of Love?

October 29

"Love one another and help others to rise to the higher levels, simply by pouring out love. Love is infectious and the greatest healing energy." Sai Baba

Grammie P

Although neither of my parents is left-handed, I am, as is one of my brothers. I vaguely remember crocheting being on the school agenda somewhere around grade 2. Because of my left-handedness, my mother was not able to teach me how to crochet or to knit. But, her mother could and did. Grammie P would sit me on her knee while she was in her rocking chair where the west fading sun would grace our hands and materials in the late afternoon. She would take my hands in hers and like teaching someone how to dance by having them stand on your feet and move with you, she would slowly and repetitiously make the stitches that would start a creation. It was fascinating to me to see individual stitches become the beginning of something creative. When I was able to manage the proper holding of the crochet hook or knitting needles, then I would sit on a wooden straight-back chair facing her in her rocking chair and I would mirror what she was doing. I still enjoy both of these hand crafts to this day and remember her patience and ability to teach me with a feeling of Love around the memories.

****

Can you think of a similar event that you can choose to perceive as a gift of Love?

_____

_____

_____

_____

_____

_____

_____

_____

_____

_____

_____

_____

_____

October 30

"Don't walk behind me; I may not lead. Don't walk in front of me; I may not follow. Just walk beside me and be my friend." Albert Camus

Carol-Anne LoP

One year, my birth daughter surprised me by sending me a package of pictures she had had done of her and her family. I was so honoured by getting this gift. Then, out of the blue, another year at Christmas, she sent a long email letter updating me on how her two girls, Sabrina and Danielle, were doing in their young lives, especially their national level winnings in synchronized swimming competitions. I have saved these special offerings as I know she has made a special effort in each case to reach out and share some of her life with me – her birth mother, even though her adopted mother is reluctant for her to have any kind of relationship with me. I know this is what Love feels like, too.

****

Can you think of a similar event that you can choose to perceive as a gift of Love?

_____

_____

_____

_____

_____

_____

_____

_____

_____

_____

_____

_____

_____

_____

October 31
"Love and magic have a great deal in common. They enrich the soul, delight the heart.
And they both take practice. " Nora Roberts

Ella F

The first year that I taught having the following summer off was a new experience instead of a regular two-week vacation time period like I always had in industry. Ten days before the end of the final semester, I asked my life-time friend if she would like to come with me and drive across Canada and back for 30 days stopping along the way and visiting with friends and relatives. She was up for the adventure and found family and friends to look after her children.

Whenever I travel, I always seem to need to record my thoughts and feelings during the event. I asked Ella to record particular details as I drove since she didn't drive. The following Christmas I received a little hard cloth-covered book that Ella had created with the story of our trip chronicled in it. This is what Love reads like.

****

Can you think of a similar event that you can choose to perceive as a gift of Love?

_____

_____

_____

_____

_____

_____

_____

_____

_____

_____

_____

_____

_____

_____

_____

November 1
"Love conquers all." Virgil

JoAnn P

As I was trying to put together information about my mother's side of the genealogy tree, I asked Mom's older sister if I could borrow her photograph albums to scan some of the older pictures of the family. JoAnn, my aunt's main care-giver daughter, was the go-between who looked after me borrowing the books, some at a time, for my project. I look on this service as an act of Love.

****

Can you think of a similar event that you can choose to perceive as a gift of Love?

_____

_____

_____

_____

_____

_____

_____

_____

_____

_____

_____

_____

_____

_____

_____

_____

November 2

"A tree is known by its fruit; a man by his deeds. A good deed is never lost; he who sows courtesy reaps friendship, and he who plants kindness gathers love." St. Basil

Sheila F

When I was actively dying in Stage IV congestive heart failure caused by untreated Graves' Disease, I was determined to die my way on my own couch in my own living room. My former student, present friend, had also become my care-giver. She came daily. She did everything for me during those 3-5 months of my "dark night of the soul." One of the caring things she did was to go to the drug store and buy elastic wraps – many packages of them, at my request. She then caringly would wrap my feet and legs to above the knees to try to slow down the progress of the fluid retention that was making my body unworkable and doing lots of damage in the process. She did this daily. This, too, is what Love feels like.

****

Can you think of a similar event that you can choose to perceive as a gift of Love?

_____

_____

_____

_____

_____

_____

_____

_____

_____

_____

_____

_____

_____

_____

November 3

"Love is what we were born with. Fear is what we learned here." Marianne Williamson

Dennis C

Somewhere around the tenth day of my start to my second time around in this lifetime, I had been moved from ICU to a private room outside a nurses' station. This is where Dennis came to visit me the day he retired and the day he flew out West to relocate with his wife's family. He came to visit me in between these two events in his life. He was very gentle with me and gave me a book with suggestions to help one live a safer and cleaner life by getting rid of toxins in our environment, food, personal care products, and water. I still have this book, have given copies to others in need, and share it when appropriate. Having been given the gift of Dennis' presence in between his two major life changes is definitely also what Love looks like.

****

Can you think of a similar event that you can choose to perceive as a gift of Love?

November 4
"Love is the foundation from which your decisions about your life should be made."
Darren L. Johnson

Linda H

The doorbell rang and when I went to see who was there, Linda was standing there smiling and had brought a friend along. When I talked about the genealogy material I was amassing and the death of a cousin's partner, Linda knew who I was talking about. She brought a relative of my cousin, who I would never have met, to meet me. Not only did she bring a lovely person into my presence, they had been cross-country skiing and she also brought some birch polypore mushrooms for their nourishing tea-making ability. Then, the two of them picked up an armload of wood and brought this in to the living room for the fire. How do you say this is what Love looks like? It should be easy by now to recognize.

****

Can you think of a similar event that you can choose to perceive as a gift of Love?

November 5

"To enlarge or illustrate this power and effect of love is to set a candle in the sun."
Robert Burton

Ella F

How great it is to share an activity with someone rather than feeling overwhelmed by the size of a task. I was attempting to put the cords of wood in the basement for use that winter. It was after the thyroid storm, after the congestive heart failure, after the atrial fibrillation, after the broken wrist, after the shattered leg that now has 10 rods and nuts and bolts in it. Twenty sticks carried two at a time from the ground up to the wheelbarrow. Push the wheelbarrow over to the basement entrance. Dump the twenty sticks down the five steps. Back to the pile of wood until there are 100 sticks in the cellar way. Now, up the 10 steps into the house, down the 13 steps to the basement, pick up two sticks at a time and carry them across the basement and stack them. Ella came on the bus and helped me whittle away at the pile of wood for a couple of hours. She didn't have to do this. She does not get any benefit from the heat this wood contributes to my welfare, but...this is another expression of Love.

****

Can you think of a similar event that you can choose to perceive as a gift of Love?

November 6

"For small creatures such as we the vastness is bearable only through love." Carl Sagan

Anne M

One August my brother and I and Anne went on a day long excursion including lunch and strolling on a beautiful sandy beach. I took some pictures and collected some rocks shaped like hearts to bring home.

The following Christmas, Anne gave me a clear dish with sand from that beach and beautiful little heart-shaped rocks that she had brought home with her from that beach we went to that past summer. This is what Love looks like, too.

****

Can you think of a similar event that you can choose to perceive as a gift of Love?

_____

_____

_____

_____

_____

_____

_____

_____

_____

_____

_____

_____

_____

_____

November 7

"Kindness in words creates confidence. Kindness in thinking creates profoundness.
Kindness in giving creates love." Lao Tzu

Don B

As I walked along the sidewalk from my house to the mail boxes, I stopped for a neighbour to leave his driveway in his half-ton pickup. He stopped and we chatted for a bit and then he brought my attention to what he had in the back of the truck. He had shot a deer, it being hunting season, and was taking his trophy to be skinned and hung and then butchered. He asked me if I liked venison to which I replied that I did.

A couple of weeks later, he arrived at my doorstep with a package of deer meat wrapped up in the brown freezer wrap paper as a gift. This is what Love tastes like.

****

Can you think of a similar event that you can choose to perceive as a gift of Love?

November 8

"Love is a canvas furnished by nature and embroidered by imagination." Voltaire

Susan B

When I put out the word that I was looking for details such as birth and death dates for relatives, Susan sent me a great email with the particulars of her parents and brother. This is what Love looks like, too.

****

Can you think of a similar event that you can choose to perceive as a gift of Love?

_____

_____

_____

_____

_____

_____

_____

_____

_____

_____

_____

_____

_____

_____

_____

_____

_____

_____

_____

_____

November 9

"Love is the joy of the good, the wonder of the wise, the amazement of the Gods." Plato

Sheila F and Jerusha Y

The day after the dark night of my soul when I asked the Universe if it was ok for me to die now and not getting a supportive feeling that I was done yet, Sheila and Jerusha came to see if they could get me out of the house and bent enough to be put in Jerusha's car for the trip to the local hospital emergency room. I had not let all my pride and ego go yet and would not allow myself to be seen by neighbours being taken by ambulance to the hospital. Sigh. What gremlins pride and ego are. After many tries and manipulations, Sheila and Jerusha finally got my body bent enough to be slid and pushed in to the passenger seat for the 10-minute drive. That took all my energy for that day. Having fluid retention up to my breast area made it very difficult to move or breathe, for that matter. Both Sheila and Jerusha made arrangements with their work requirements to make this happen. Another life-saving act of Love.

****

Can you think of a similar event that you can choose to perceive as a gift of Love?

November 10
"To fear love is to fear life, and those who fear life are already three parts dead."
Bertrand Russell

Dr. Jenni M
When we were not able to get the inflammation in my body down to an acceptable level through nutrition and homeopathic remedies, Dr. Jenni suggested I make contact with Denise who carried a product called Wobenzym. I would never have known about Denise or her little shop with specialty health-enhancing products. Sharing this information is also what Love sounds like.
****

Can you think of a similar event that you can choose to perceive as a gift of Love?

November 11

"Hatred does not cease through hatred at any time. Hatred ceases through love. This is an unalterable law." Buddha

Ian P

When I saw Ian at a friend's place, I asked him if he would share where he got his sauna. He said it was expensive and he thought that there was a local supplier that carried a similar sauna with the same ceramic heater for much less money. Since Ian paid quite a bit of money for his sauna, he certainly did not have to share there was an alternative that I might like to check. This, too, is what Love does.

****

Can you think of a similar event that you can choose to perceive as a gift of Love?

November 12
"The hunger for love is much more difficult to remove than the hunger for bread."
Mother Teresa

Sarah H

When my car dragged me down the rough dirt embankment with one leg shattered and the other under the car, I knew I could not let go of the car or my leg under the car would also be damaged. I heard a voice from far away saying, "Do you need help?" I said yes I did. Immediately, this lithe young mother of a little baby she was carrying came running down the hill to where I was hanging on to the car. I immediately said, "Lean in over me and..." to which she interjected that she couldn't drive a standard shift car. I continued, "and pull the emergency brake so I can let go of the car." She immediately did this and then said she was going for help. I watched her run back up the side of the hill to where a maroon passenger van was just pulling in to a parking space. She went to the driver and said I needed help and they came. Since I was in and out of consciousness on the slide down the hill, I can't imagine why Sarah thought to look in my direction – away from the store to which she was heading – or why she thought to shout whether I needed help or not – and to finally be the first responder to my latest learning experience, but she did all these things and I am so, so grateful. This is what Love does unbidden and without fanfare or expectation.

****

Can you think of a similar event that you can choose to perceive as a gift of Love?

_____

_____

_____

_____

_____

_____

_____

_____

_____

_____

_____

_____

November 13

"A friend is one who knows you and loves you just the same." Elbert Hubbard

Bob H

When I was in the throes of congestive heart failure and still thinking (because I was not able to think clearly) I could do whatever I wanted to do when I wanted to do it, I was trying to clear alder bush roots away from the driveway to my little piece of land on the shore. Ferne was helping and when Bob asked what I was doing, I told him we were digging roots up from the path at the shore land. He said he would come and help. He did. It was August and it was hot and it was back-breaking work. I stood around and tried to get my breath while they worked. Bob offering to help made the job go twice as fast so that we could get the car in and out without tearing the underbelly of the car off or puncturing the tires. Bob's labour, freely given, is also what Love looks like.

****

Can you think of a similar event that you can choose to perceive as a gift of Love?

November 14
"Sometimes the heart sees what is invisible to the eye." H. Jackson Brown, Jr.

Annette S and Kathy B

That fateful day when I thought I was Superman's sister and attempted to stop a rolling car from sliding down a hill, just as the first angel named Sarah and her baby came to offer help, a second maroon van was driving in to another parking space up on the hill at the gas station. When Sarah ran up and asked if they might be able to help, Annette and her sister, Kathy, immediately came running down to where I was on the ground in and out of consciousness. Annette was a nurse. How provident was that for me! She insisted that I needed to go to hospital although ego was still alive and kicking at the seams in my monkey mind and when I was conscious, I was arguing I wanted to go home and I would ice my leg in the bathtub.

Common sense and nursing acumen prevailed so that when my neighbour, Philip, arrived to pick up his mail, too, Annette and Kathy (who just 'happened' to have a wheelchair in their van) got me up off the ground and in to Philip's car. Annette and Kathy were not from this area and did not know where the hospital was, but Philip did, so off we went. Annette and Kathy being there, obviously by divine providence, provided the exact type of Love that was needed just then. I am so grateful.

****

Can you think of a similar event that you can choose to perceive as a gift of Love?

_____

_____

_____

_____

_____

_____

_____

_____

_____

_____

_____

_____

November 15
"Nobody has ever measured, not even poets, how much the heart can hold."
Zelda Fitzgerald

Helga J

When I arrived in Toronto five months' pregnant, I first met a high school friend who was living with her brother and working there. That first night we slept on their living room floor (it was the 60s!) and even though I did not arrive until after 2 a.m., we talked well in to the night. She was astonished that I was pregnant, in Toronto alone, and asking her if we could find a place to live together. She agreed to all this and we became the best of roommates for almost a year. She was my rock and my pillow because we were living in a basement apartment in a private house that had one large bed so we slept together. When it came time to have my baby, she and her brother who had the car, took me to the hospital.

She was the perfect act of Love that I needed at that time to allow me to live through this very large traumatic and life-changing period of my life. I will never forget her kindness.

****

Can you think of a similar event that you can choose to perceive as a gift of Love?

_____

_____

_____

_____

_____

_____

_____

_____

_____

_____

_____

_____

_____

November 16
"Love... it surrounds every being and extends slowly to embrace all that shall be."
Khalil Gibran

Flo B

Aunt Flo was Mom's sister. She had the most engaging laugh. Her face would light up when she laughed. One time when I was home visiting from Ontario, I went to visit her. She was cleaning out some things in her attic. One of the things she was going to throw away was what looked like an old-fashioned, probably 1930-40's coat. I asked if I might have it. She said of course.

I took the coat back to Toronto and took it to a furrier to see about having it updated from the large bulky arms and front, asking the furrier if it was worth fixing. He looked at me and said with much distain that I did not know that this coat was a "Mouton" and, of course, it was worth it. I still have this gift and think of Aunt Flo whenever I put it on or see it hanging in my closet. This is what Love feel like – very warm and cozy.

****

Can you think of a similar event that you can choose to perceive as a gift of Love?

_____

_____

_____

_____

_____

_____

_____

_____

_____

_____

_____

_____

_____

_____

November 17
"There is only one terminal dignity - love." Helen Hayes

Glenne P

One day I got a call from Aunt Glenne. She wanted to tell me that she thought I was doing a great job of helping Mom in the different ways that I was to help make her life somewhat better in her difficult aging years. I was so appreciative of this phone call and still remember how I felt the Love coming through the phone to wrap me in a warm cocoon.

****

Can you think of a similar event that you can choose to perceive as a gift of Love?

November 18
"Looking back, I have this to regret, that too often when I loved, I did not say so."
David Grayson

Les O

After Les and Tracy left Tigger here and went on their way to Texas for Tracy to do her Ph.D. in education leadership, it was a year before they came back to visit. On that visit, Les had these malleable eye glasses that looked so comfortable that I asked where did he get them. He said he got them at a dollar store and whipped them off his face and handed them to me. When I tried them and found the strength the same as what I needed, I handed them back. He said for me to keep them as he had several others. This is what Love does – gives you the shirt off its back – or in this case, the glasses off his face. I am wearing them now to proofread this page.

****

Can you think of a similar event that you can choose to perceive as a gift of Love?

_____

_____

_____

_____

_____

_____

_____

_____

_____

_____

_____

_____

_____

_____

_____

November 19
"There is no remedy for love but to love more." Henry David Thoreau

Carol G

At one point in my career, I was living over an hour away from where I was working. When I asked an uncle if I might stay at their house during the week for a couple of months, the answer was yes. Carol, my aunt, chose which bedroom of her children who were away from home, that I would inhabit. Her choice was impeccable for my broader knowledge of classical literature as on the headboard, there was a soft cover book entitled, "The Song of Roland" about Charlemagne's time in French history. What a treasure! On that headboard were Russian fairy tales to delight the senses, too. Carol's choice of which room I could stay in resulted in a new exposure to literature that I do not believe I would ever have had, had she not chosen so well for me. This, too, is what Love reads like.

****

Can you think of a similar event that you can choose to perceive as a gift of Love?

November 20
"Love seeketh not itself to please, but for another gives its ease." William Blake

Alex P

I first started talking about writing this book-type journal when I was still partaking of Jerusha's monthly women's salon pot luck suppers. Alex was one of the people to whom I waxed about my dream for its fulfillment. She is the one who suggested that I make the book a type of workbook so people could become engaged in the process, too.

This is why this journal has become the format that it is. Love, by the name of Alex, suggested an enhancement that has made all the difference in its creation and utility.

****

Can you think of a similar event that you can choose to perceive as a gift of Love?

November 21
"To understand everything is to forgive everything." Buddha

Dennis C

One of the requirements in order to be accepted for the university Ph.D. program in metaphysics, was several letters of reference. I asked Dennis since he had known be for more than 20 years. He wrote the most succinct and glowing letter that I still have it posted on the front of my fridge all these years later. Perhaps this is something we should all do once every ten or twenty years – ask a trusted friend to write a reference letter for us and give us a copy so we can see how an other might see us as a sort of affirmation. This act is also what Love reads like.

****

Can you think of a similar event that you can choose to perceive as a gift of Love?

_____

_____

_____

_____

_____

_____

_____

_____

_____

_____

_____

_____

_____

_____

_____

November 22
"It is not so much our friends' help that helps us, as the confidence of their help."
Epicurus

Binnie L
Binnie taught computer science at the local community college where I also taught more of the soft skills in communication, organizational behaviour, management principles, and human relations. He has always been the most straight-up person I know. What you see is what you get – there are no surprises – and what you get is kindness, always kindness.

When I was mentioning to Binnie and his wife, Wanda, about the snow drifting in to my bedroom through the old aluminum storm door and ill-fitting wooden house door, he offered to replace not only the aluminum storm door on the bedroom but also the one on the front door of the house if I would get the doors. He then went to the trouble of finding good doors on sale at a local hardware store and letting me know their stock numbers for ordering plus the actual sizes I needed.

When I got the doors, Binnie came and took off the old doors and installed the new doors. He would not think of taking any compensation for this work. This is also what Love feels like since there now is no more snow drifting in to my bedroom!

****

Can you think of a similar event that you can choose to perceive as a gift of Love?

_____

_____

_____

_____

_____

_____

_____

_____

_____

_____

_____

_____

_____

November 23

"To love is so startling it leaves little time for anything else." Emily Dickinson

Donna R

Donna and I both taught business math at the local community college. Sometimes we would go on drives around the area looking to see what was 'over the mountain'. When I mentioned to her I was looking for an upright piano, she knew of one for sale and gave me the contact information. I still have that beautiful Heinzman piano that sounds so wonderful. I thank her for this gift every time I pass by it, or on the infrequent times when I actually sit and play. This is what Love sounds like.

****

Can you think of a similar event that you can choose to perceive as a gift of Love?

November 24
"All a sane man can ever think about is giving love." Hafiz [Sufi Mystic and Poet]

Rodney S

Facilitating adult students' learning to be employable encompasses hard skills such as computer literacy and accounting, and soft skills such as communications, human relations and organizational behaviour. Rodney was taking accounting and one of the required soft courses was organizational behaviour. He would challenge me almost every day whenever a topic came up where the choices for action were not cast in stone or black and white, but were more than sixty shades of grey. He was always solicitous; however, he really wanted a yes or no answer to situations where one had to use common sense and one's own ethical moral base to make the best educated guess as to what was appropriate within context in a particular situation. He was so uncomfortable with this total opposite to his other right/wrong courses he was taking.

Several years after he finished the program, I met him in a store in his area of the province. He was determined to have me understand that he now realized how important the soft skills I was trying to get him to pay attention to were in his life, that he was so thankful he had been challenged by me and that I wouldn't let him off the hook to do his absolute best. Many lesser personalities would never admit such a revelation and his sharing of his awakening to the need for these soft skills is also another successful course in Love.

****

Can you think of a similar event that you can choose to perceive as a gift of Love?

_____

_____

_____

_____

_____

_____

_____

_____

_____

_____

_____

_____

_____

November 25
"Love is the first ingredient in the relief of suffering."
Padre Pio [Cappuchin priest, mystic, confessor, stigmatic 1887-1968. For 50 years he suffered the five wounds of the crucifixion.]

Beverly P

We met at my first office job with the Department of National Defense. After I moved to Toronto, he was stationed in Cyprus and Lebanon for a couple of years during the 1960s. He and I would write letters during his time overseas. In one letter I received, he had enclosed a gold cross on a chain. Today that item in a letter envelope would never make it through the postal system; however, then, it did. When he came back from his tour, he stopped in to see me in Toronto. He was war-ravaged with what today would have been diagnosed as PTSD. He went on with his life, moving back to his original location where he grew up and I continued on with my life with its learning opportunities, too. I still have that gold chain and cross. It is another physical example of what Love looks like.

****

Can you think of a similar event that you can choose to perceive as a gift of Love?

November 26
"What is man's ultimate direction in life? It is to look for love, truth, virtue, and beauty."
Shinichi Suzuki

Wendy T
Finding someone who is willing and interested in listening to one's stories while also sharing theirs is always a special occasion. Wendy pops in to my life for a couple of hours at a time and we always have the most interesting discourse on such topics as parallel realities, mystical experiences, mundane trials and tribulations of our little immediate lives, as well as adventurous stuff like where will be look for signs of archaeological historical origins within our own space and time. This fellow traveler's conjoining with my own interests is also what Love looks like.
****

Can you think of a similar event that you can choose to perceive as a gift of Love?

_____

_____

_____

_____

_____

_____

_____

_____

_____

_____

_____

_____

_____

_____

_____

November 27
"When someone loves you, the way they say your name is different. You know that your name is safe in their mouth." Child, age 4

John C

Every time I was called to my division manager's office, my immediate thought was that I had done something wrong for which I would be fired. You know, living in the irrational FEAR box? One day, he called me on it. When I arrived at his office, he said, "Are your palms sweaty? Is your heart racing? Are you afraid you are going to be reprimanded or even fired?" What could I say to these questions? He had named my elephant that I carried around on my shoulders. I had always felt I would be found out a fraud and ridiculed for it somehow.

He was very gentle and said, "You are doing a great job as manager of the administrative services here. However, I am going to suggest that you consider finding a way to go to university so that you do not feel inferior to others who have university degrees – and I am going to suggest that you consider finding a way to go back home and make peace with your past." How can I talk about this little 'talk' without knowing that it was one of the biggest gifts in my life? For the next year, he made space in my working day to attend university as a pre-student taking one class to see if I could actually succeed if I enrolled fulltime. Then, when I put in my resignation and told him I was moving back to the province from where I came, he said he would find it hard to replace me (he hired two people to do what I was doing), but that he felt I would benefit greatly from this decision. Love comes in so many disguises and this one was a doozie.

****

Can you think of a similar event that you can choose to perceive as a gift of Love?

_____

_____

_____

_____

_____

_____

_____

_____

_____

_____

_____

November 28

"I have friends in overalls whose friendship I would not swap for the favor of the kings of the world." Thomas A. Edison

Chuck Z

Charles came in to my life in my Grade 10 class part way through the year. Within months, he was courting my sister. They were each other's best friend and lived in each other's pocket. They married, had one child, and played golf and travelled. Chuck and a friend opened an automotive parts business in the city. Whenever I needed new tires, brake shoes or pads, a muffler, oil and air filter, Chuck would bring them to me and charge me a reduced price. Just because he was my brother-in law, he didn't have to personally deliver these automotive items to wherever I happened to be living – but he did. This is what Love does.

****

Can you think of a similar event that you can choose to perceive as a gift of Love?

_____

_____

_____

_____

_____

_____

_____

_____

_____

_____

_____

_____

_____

_____

November 29
"There is a wisdom of the head, and a wisdom of the heart." Charles Dickens

Shelley M

Shelley's husband, Ted, was stricken with brain cancer in his mid 50s. Although I no longer worked with them, Shelley continued to keep me informed of important news about former colleagues. As Ted's journey included multiple rounds of chemotherapy, loss of memory and coordination, as he moved through home care to palliative care, Shelley was stalwart faithful to her husband's quest for meaning of his life by regularly sending emails to update me of his triumphs and setbacks. She did this up to and including his death less than two years later. This strength of character, courage to honour her husband's life and journey, and commitment to communicate to make meaning because it was her journey, too, is definitely a glimpse of what Love looks like.

****

Can you think of a similar event that you can choose to perceive as a gift of Love?

November 30
"A loving heart is the beginning of all knowledge." Thomas Carlyle

Brenda D and Stephen L

While having tenants in the upstairs apartment for almost ten years, the plaster around the chimney going from the roof to the basement for the oil furnace, became more and more unsightly with rust stains from a slow leak of water at the roof level. After the tenants moved, I attempted to find where the problem was in order to have it corrected. I had trades people come, masons, roofers, carpenters. None of them ever went up on the roof to look closely, although many went up the ladder to look at the chimney as it came through the attic.

Brenda, bless her agile body, not only went up the ladder to the attic, she also took materials and conducted a test to see just where the water was seeping down the chimney – on which side, by taping paper towel to the bricks all around it. From time to time, she would go up to the attic, climb up on the rafters, and check it diligently.

When we finally felt we had found the problem area, a neighbour and roofer, Stephen, not only came, he also went up on the roof with another worker, found the gap, and filled it. This determination to get to the bottom of a problem to help another, specifically me, is also what Love looks like.

****

Can you think of a similar event that you can choose to perceive as a gift of Love?

_____

_____

_____

_____

_____

_____

_____

_____

_____

_____

_____

_____

_____

December 1
"Love consists in this, that two solitudes protect and touch and greet each other."
Rainer Maria Rilke

Julie M

Virginia and I were slotted as roommates by Julia Cameron when we attended the creativity workshop in Taos, New Mexico. Spending a week in one another's company, we became friends. Even though we did not see each other very often, we corresponded the old-fashioned way, that is, long-hand letter – how wonderful!

When I had not heard from Virginia for over a year, I wondered how she was doing. It wasn't very long after this that I got a letter in the mail from Julie, one of Virginia's daughters. Virginia's breast cancer from many years ago had returned and she had died. I felt a deep loss at this news. Then, in the next mail delivery came this large portfolio-sized envelope from Julie. It was one of her mother's watercolour paintings of the surrounding mesa that she loved so much and painted continuously. Julie said that Virginia talked of our friendship often and she felt I would like one of her mother's pieces of art. Love from a distance, unbidden, totally appreciated.
****

Can you think of a similar event that you can choose to perceive as a gift of Love?

December 2
"Love consists in this, that two solitudes protect and touch and greet each other."
Rainer Maria Rilke

Rev. Sam B

About a year after my husband and I separated, I got a call from his mother saying that he had tried to commit suicide, was in hospital, and it was all my fault. I tried to fathom out what to do or not do with this information and finally called my husband's maternal uncle in the States who also happened to be a minister. When I told Sam about the telephone call from his sister, he became very silent for some time on the line.

Finally, he hesitantly said that if I chose to go back in to the marriage under these conditions, then I would be, proverbially, under my husband's thumb, and any time something difficult came up in the relationship, he could threaten suicide attempts to gain his way. I thought about this counseling for a long time and finally decided that he had given me the best gift of impartial advice in the situation. This, too, is what Love sounds like.

****

Can you think of a similar event that you can choose to perceive as a gift of Love?

_____

_____

_____

_____

_____

_____

_____

_____

_____

_____

_____

_____

_____

December 3

"In our life there is a single color, as on an artist's palette, which provides the meaning of life and art. It is the color of love." Marc Chagall

Karen W

Richard Hatfield of New Brunswick made the comment in the late 1980s/early 1990s that, yes, he had imbibed of the weed, but he had never inhaled. What a crock! I lived in Toronto during the 1960s and 1970s. Friday nights were spent in Yorkville taking in the music entertainment and attending parties at Rochdale College on Yonge Street. However, I never smoked nor inhaled of the weed until I was in my 61st year. It was not something that I felt I needed to do. When I turned 60 years of age, you might say, it was on my bucket list. I know, I know, funny. If I hadn't tried it by then, why now? Well, to see what other people found so interesting, of course. On a long weekend, Karen came dressed with wide-bottomed-leg psychedelic skinny pants, a scarf tied around her head, a suede coat with fringes hanging from the underarms, and three long-playing records of Woodstock – and the prerequisite package. Needless to say, we inhaled. She danced and laughed and I had another one of my sleep paralysis episodes. This one lasted for six hours. Karen never left my side, at least for long. She would rake leaves, talk on the phone, dance, laugh, ask me if I needed anything or how I was doing and played the records. When I finally was released from my stupor safe and sound, but tired, we hugged and she went on her way home. This was a huge demonstration of what Love smells and feels like, for which I now know I don't have to wonder any more. It has been experienced so that can be crossed off my list.

****

Can you think of a similar event that you can choose to perceive as a gift of Love?

_____

_____

_____

_____

_____

_____

_____

_____

_____

_____

December 4
"Love is what makes you smile when you're tired." Child, age 6

Daddy G

One night, when I was maybe five or six years old, Dad and I were walking from his mother's house to our house 'across the way'. It was late Fall and it was dark there not being any outside lights in this small village – and only oil lamps lighting the interior of most of the houses. Dad had my hand in his great big one and we were walking along. The stars in the sky were twinkling. I pointed and asked about a certain constellation, since I always had 'why' questions when I was very young. Having been a fisherman, Dad knew about the constellations and pointed out Orion and all the stars that showed the shoulders, the knees and, especially the belt. Orion is my favourite constellation. My star constellation of Love.

****

Can you think of a similar event that you can choose to perceive as a gift of Love?

_____

_____

_____

_____

_____

_____

_____

_____

_____

_____

_____

_____

_____

_____

_____

December 5
"To love another person is to see the face of God. [Les Miserables]" Victor Hugo

Sonny H and Michael I

Lloyd invited me over by boat to his island for lobster one Sunday. We left about 9:30 a.m. The open boat had a small motor, no life jackets, and no pail with which to bail water. Lloyd did not seem to mind any of these limitations, probably because in his lifetime he had been involved in the dorey boat races between Massachusetts and Nova Scotia where he and his crew had won many a year.

The five miles of Atlantic Ocean was choppy with the boat having some sort of leaky bottom since by the time we got to the island, there was about 8 inches of water in it. Maybe this was normal? I didn't know. All I knew was when Lloyd drove the boat up on the sand at the island, I wanted off. I walked up to the brow of the boat and jumped the five to six feet onto what I thought was the soft sand.

The sand was like cement. I broke my leg just above the ankle. Since I had never had a broken bone, I didn't know how much pain it would cause and thought maybe it was sprained. I hobbled up the hill to the house and we proceeded to spend the day while my leg and foot became blacker and bigger by the hour. Rum helped, but not enough. By the time Lloyd's son, Sonny, arrived about 4 p.m., I begged him to immediately take me in his boat back over to the mainland. He did. When we got to the wharf, his friend and my acquaintance, Michael was there in his truck talking with other fishermen. Sonny called for Michael to come help get me out of the boat and up the wharf ladder as the tide was mostly out meaning there were more stairs to climb. Michael was very helpful and drove me to the hospital where they x-rayed and sent me home, also thinking it was sprained. Since I was also working at the hospital for the Director at that time, I was in to work the next day. It was not until four days later that my physician came to find me to tell me the leg was broken and I needed to come to emergency so he could set it and cast it. Sonny and Michael were my two angels that Sunday afternoon. This, too, is what Love does.

****

Can you think of a similar event that you can choose to perceive as a gift of Love?

_____

_____

_____

_____

_____

_____

_____

_____

_____

_____

December 6
"The idea is to write it so that people hear it and it slides through the brain and goes straight to the heart." Maya Angelou

Robbie S

Jerusha gave me a DVD of a particular kind of yoga that I was interested in learning. When I couldn't get the DVD to work, I asked Robbie if he could reprogram it so I could. Robbie has special computer knowledge and skills that are invaluable. He kindly fixed whatever the problem was and I can now view the DVD's contents. This is what Love does, too.

****

Can you think of a similar event that you can choose to perceive as a gift of Love?

_____

_____

_____

_____

_____

_____

_____

_____

_____

_____

_____

_____

_____

_____

_____

_____

_____

_____

December 7
"It's the friends you can call up at 4 a.m. that matter." Marlene Dietrich

Dr. Lois H

After I left the hospital from the near death experience, I had promised myself that if I lived it would not be on any more prescription drugs than was absolutely necessary – a commitment I made to myself in my early 20s. To this end, I made an appointment with Dr. Lois, a naturopath. She was ever so helpful. She suggested alternative remedies to the heavy-duty drugs I was on for my heart. Over the next three years, I gradually was weaned off all the drugs that I left the hospital with in my survival kitbag. Dr. Lois helped tremendously with this beginning quest for knowledge to learn how to take care of my health and wellbeing. She role-played what Love looks like.

****

Can you think of a similar event that you can choose to perceive as a gift of Love?

December 8
"We know that we have passed from death into life, because we love... [1 John 3:14]"
Bible

Dr. Russell G

That summer Russell drove his Porsche Targa Florio home the 1200 miles with his wife and their luggage to play golf all scrunched in the little two-seater. He ordered the car when he was stationed in Germany with the military. Loving to drive a standard shift car, I asked if I might drive it. He said only if he came along, too. Off we went.

When I was married to my formula-racing husband, I drove our Porsche, too. This was different. We were in the country, not the city, and there were long stretches without stop signs or encumbrances. It drove beautifully and I drove it very, very quick, as they say in the formula racing industry. Russell suggested I might slow down since we were becoming airborne. He never shouted at me or grabbed the wheel. He let me wind her out, so they say. This is what Love feels like, too.

****

Can you think of a similar event that you can choose to perceive as a gift of Love?

_____

_____

_____

_____

_____

_____

_____

_____

_____

_____

_____

_____

_____

_____

December 9

"Show me your hands. Do they have scars from giving? Show me your feet. Are they wounded in service? Show me your heart. Have you left a place for divine love?"
Fulton J. Sheen

Ellen S

I met Ellen through another friend. She was having some lung problems; however, she was engaging, tried QiGong with me, went to a local spiritual meeting with me, told me about her skills in emotional freedom tapping and with whom she studied, about her students in Ontario and her partner's e-book he was writing. Then, she said she had also published a book and gave me a copy. I was thrilled and amazed. This is what Love looks like.

****

Can you think of a similar event that you can choose to perceive as a gift of Love?

_____

_____

_____

_____

_____

_____

_____

_____

_____

_____

_____

_____

_____

_____

_____

_____

_____

_____

December 10

"But friendship is precious, not only in the shade, but in the sunshine of life, and thanks to a benevolent arrangement the greater part of life is sunshine." Thomas Jefferson

Lee P

When my uncle Leander asked me if I could find out what happened to his father's other children by his first wife, I am sure neither he nor I had any idea of the honey hole I was about to enter. Genealogy is totally addicting. The more you find out about your roots, the more you want to know. It took me over a year of searching; however, with the help of anonymous distant relatives in the United States, I was able to give him answers. He could have had no idea when he asked the question, trusting I would be able to help him, how much pleasure he has given me and the project continues to call and give me more rewards. This is how Love works, too.

****

Can you think of a similar event that you can choose to perceive as a gift of Love?

December 11
"You change your life by changing your heart." Max Lucado

Grendel and Virginia E

Virginia invited me to visit at her place just outside Santa Fe in New Mexico. I loved going to visit with her. I loved her choices of decorations within her home, her artwork hung on the walls, the adobe structures, the little pine trees and cholla plants all around, the wide expanses with the big sky.

I had been particularly tired before embarking on this trip and by the time I flew in to Albuquerque, rented a car, and drove the two hours up the 4,000 feet elevation to the edge of the mountains, I was exhausted. I lay down on my bed for my week's stay and proceeded to become comatose for the next three days.

Grendel was Virginia's elder dog. She never left my side. She lay on the mat in front of the bed where I had, what I guess must have been altitude sickness, although I was not sick to my stomach, just not able to get up or stay awake. Grendel never waivered in her vigil and I recovered. Virginia would check on me, but let Nature take its natural course until I rejoined her. What a gift of Love both Virginia and Grendel have been in my life.

****

Can you think of a similar event that you can choose to perceive as a gift of Love?

_____

_____

_____

_____

_____

_____

_____

_____

_____

_____

_____

_____

December 12
"It matters not
Who you love
Where you love
Why you love
When you love
Or how you love
It matters only that you love."
John Lennon

Melissa M

After having two of the upstairs rooms painted out and they just looking so darn good, I was musing to Melissa that maybe I would have the great room, alcove and closet painted out in the Spring. Melissa said, "I'll do it. I like painting." I was astounded. This was a huge job because the plaster had to have holes and cracks repaired and filled and sanded, the ceiling had to be done – and anyone who has ever painted, knows how strong your abdominal core muscles have to be to do that, the trim around the windows and doors and the wallboards all had to be primed and painted, too.

I told her I didn't think I was worthy of her offer, which I truly felt was overwhelming in its generosity. You see, there I was, back in the Fear bucket, argh! She said my statement made her want to cry.

Over the next couple of months, she came and picked away at the massive project and did the most outstandingly beautiful work I could never have hired. My heart has opened more with this gift of Love, the shutters are permanently nailed away from the panes of light so that others' light shines in on me – and my light is allowed to shine out on the world. This is definitely another hue of what Love looks like.

****

Can you think of a similar event that you can choose to perceive as a gift of Love?

_____

_____

_____

_____

_____

_____

_____

_____

December 13

"Darkness cannot drive out darkness; only light can do that. Hate cannot drive out hate; only love can do that." Martin Luther King, Jr.

Chris and Vicki M

How can I position Vicki in my genealogy? She is the daughter of my first cousin. Does that make her my second cousin? Probably. She asked me to be the official photographer at her wedding. Whenever I photographed weddings, especially of relatives, I always found it very emotionally difficult to maintain a professional stance while also being part of the festivities. I guess I was still in the Fear bucket, afraid of making a mistake that could not be reshot after the fact. Chris and Vicki were absolutely gracious in accepting whatever images I had taken as totally great. This is what Love does, too.

****

Can you think of a similar event that you can choose to perceive as a gift of Love?

December 14
"Love is, above all, the gift of oneself." Jean Anouilh

Jim D

As many of my new-found avenues to wellness have come through Jerusha, so, too, has Jim. Jim has the unique talent to read people's health needs and the special ability to provide energy frequencies that help one's cellular structures come back in to resonance with the rest of the body. When I asked Jim what I might do to help myself, he gave me a list of frequency numbers so that I could use them like mantras to repeat during the day because thinking of the numbers will also give them power to work at the energetic level of the body. He is giving me his trade secrets when he shares specific number sequences for me to work with in between our shared times together. He trusts me. This is what Love does.

****

Can you think of a similar event that you can choose to perceive as a gift of Love?

_____

_____

_____

_____

_____

_____

_____

_____

_____

_____

_____

_____

_____

_____

_____

December 15
"There is nothing stronger in the world than gentleness." Han Suyin

Anne M

It has been a long time challenge clawing my way back to some semblance of health after ten years of neglect and abuse. One time I saw Anne, she was wearing the most unusual necklace and bracelet that looked like woven rope of a sort with lumps of something interspersed. I asked her about them and she told me they were magnetic and helped one's electrical energy to flow better. She was a distributor for the product and would be glad to let me use her account to order if I chose. I did. I wear them – and when I do, my energy level increases significantly. This is what Love feels like! Some say it is the power of suggestion – who cares? as long as it works!

****

Can you think of a similar event that you can choose to perceive as a gift of Love?

_____

_____

_____

_____

_____

_____

_____

_____

_____

_____

_____

_____

_____

_____

December 16

"My friends, love is better than anger. Hope is better than fear. Optimism is better than despair. So let us be loving, hopeful and optimistic. And we'll change the world."
Jack Layton

Chas G

Gifts come in every shape and dimension. Some may not look like gifts; however, upon reflection, most experiences are, in fact, all experiences are, learning opportunities, to learn about the varieties of love. Chas got a phone call while visiting me. It was a strained conversation that upset. I got to vicariously experience how one actually expresses anger, frustration, betrayal, and disappointment verbally. This has been a huge lesson for me as most of my life I have swallowed and buried my hurts instead of speaking my truth and naming my feelings. This learning experience was a huge lesson for me. Unbeknownst to Chas, I got another opportunity to receive Love by proximity – a huge gift for me in my journey.

****

Can you think of a similar event that you can choose to perceive as a gift of Love?

December 17
"There are two ways of spreading light: to be the candle or the mirror that reflects it."
Edith Wharton

Maureen P

At a monthly women's only pot luck, I met Maureen, a retired social worker. We exchanged discussion of where we were from, what we had done so far in our lives, what we were doing now, and who we might know in common. The route to find common ground. One of the host's feline friends came through the room and Maureen bent down to call and pet one of the local feline residents. Then she told me a wonderful piece of information, she had noticed that whenever and where ever she used the word, "lovely" in calling a cat she did not know, the cat would always come and purr and rub up against her. She felt they particularly like the sound of the word. Why wouldn't they? It has as its root the word "love." What a lovely story to share. This is what Love sounds like. Prrrrr.

****

Can you think of a similar event that you can choose to perceive as a gift of Love?

December 18

"Lots of people want to ride with you in the limo, but what you want is someone who will take the bus with you when the limo breaks down." Oprah Winfrey

Les O and Dr. Tracy E

That year after having my life saved and having broken my wrist, but before shattering my leg, I wanted to renew my contract with life, so I booked a month-long train trip out West. The farthest I went was to visit Les and Tracy which included renting a car and driving six to seven hours to get to their place.

They had invited friends of theirs over and Les had made a lovely roast beef dinner for the occasion. I was feted. During the couple of days that I stayed, Tracy would suggest places to visit to get a feel for the surrounding area while she was at work and I could mosey around on my own. I saw wondrous places and things and met great people. This is what Love does, too.

****

Can you think of a similar event that you can choose to perceive as a gift of Love?

_____

_____

_____

_____

_____

_____

_____

_____

_____

_____

_____

_____

_____

_____

December 19
"Love is my religion - I could die for it." John Keats

Vince Y

The porter on the overnight train from Halifax to Montreal's name was Vince. He treated me like royalty. Maybe the cast from the tips of my fingers to my elbow had something to do with it? He carried my backpack. He got me bottled water. He allowed me to sleep all day if I was feeling tired with the curtain drawn. He brought me the newspaper. He made arrangements ahead of time so that when I arrived in Montreal, there was an attendant with a wheelchair waiting to take me to my next train platform. He made arrangements that this continued to happen throughout the almost 30-day trip that I took as my re-entry into this second life I have been given to experience. This is what Love looks like, too.

****

Can you think of a similar event that you can choose to perceive as a gift of Love?

December 20
"Hatred paralyzes life; love releases it. Hatred confuses life; love harmonizes it. Hatred darkens life; love illumines it." Martin Luther King

Joanne D

Every once in a very long while, years apart, I get a phone call from out West. Joanne is on the other end. She was an adult student of mine almost thirty years ago. She still calls and updates me on what is happening in her life. This is what Love sounds like.

****

Can you think of a similar event that you can choose to perceive as a gift of Love?

_____

_____

_____

_____

_____

_____

_____

_____

_____

_____

_____

_____

_____

_____

_____

_____

_____

_____

December 21
"You really shouldn't say "I love you" unless you mean it. But if you mean it, you should say it a lot. People forget." Child, age 5

Nova P

Nova calls me grandmother. In reading why spiders were coming in to my life, both literally and figuratively, sometimes biting me, sometimes just sitting and looking at me from my car dash, I see that spiders are thought to weave the web from past to future using the spiral form. They are also considered to be the embodiment of creativity and the alphabet. Whenever I forget to write, then I have a spider dream, or one is walking across the couch that I am lounging in, or I get bitten by one. I am supposed to be dreaming the web and this is why Nova calls me grandmother. I did not know this until I reread that the spider symbolizes the grandmother or crone wisdom. Thank you, Nova. This is what Love sounds like, too.

****

Can you think of a similar event that you can choose to perceive as a gift of Love?

December 22

"Give expression to the noble desires that lie in your heart." Gordon B. Hinckley

Bill W

Bill was also an adult student coming back to college to upgrade his skills. He put huge amounts of time and effort in to his assignments and it showed in his stellar marks. At the end of the semester, he brought me a gift. He had gone shad fishing and had filleted one and gave it to me ready to be cooked and eaten. I had never tasted shad before. It is exquisite in its delicacy. What a powerful taste of Love.

****

Can you think of a similar event that you can choose to perceive as a gift of Love?

_____

_____

_____

_____

_____

_____

_____

_____

_____

_____

_____

_____

_____

_____

_____

_____

_____

_____

December 23

"When I say, "I love you," it's not because I want you or because I can't have you. It has nothing to do with me. I love what you are, what you do, how you try. I've seen your kindness and your strength. I've seen the best and the worst of you. And I understand with perfect clarity exactly what you are. You're a hell of a person." Joss Whedon

Chris H

Chris was one of those persons who come in to your life for a season and/or for a reason only to move on again after his mission is accomplished. In one of our deep sharing conversations I told him about my birth daughter living in another province and how I wondered how she was doing. He immediately became very agitated and leapt up and down, saying, "You have to find her! You have to find her now! This is the most important thing you should be doing in your life." Of course, he was right. The Universe had brought him in to my life just for this purpose – to remind me of my purpose at that point in time.

When I contacted the Children's Aid Society, lo and behold, my birth daughter was also looking for me. At that time, they could do nothing with a one-sided request for information unless both parties were interested in reuniting. Since both of us had contacted them independently, we started the arduous journey to meeting each other as adults and wending our way through the perils of our reunion. Chris's insistence that I do my part is what Love sounds like.

****

Can you think of a similar event that you can choose to perceive as a gift of Love?

_____

_____

_____

_____

_____

_____

_____

_____

_____

_____

_____

_____

December 24
"Love is metaphysical gravity." R. Buckminster Fuller

Tim Horton's clerk

I went in to the Tim Horton's to get a coffee. As I was standing in the line waiting, I thought about the couple of people I had invited in after we went to church on Christmas Eve for the carol-singing. I thought perhaps I should also get a couple of cookies to share. When I went to pay, I only had a gift card that I could not remember how much money was available on it. I gave the card to the clerk and said that there might not be enough money to cover everything, in which case, I would only take the coffee. She would not tell me how much money was left on the gift card, nor how much the total for the selected items was. Instead, she said she also had a card that she would use to make up the difference. This is a large multi-franchised corporation. I was amazed that she was giving me this unsolicited gift. When she was through, I asked her if she had been hugged yet that day and when she said 'no', I asked her to come around the counter so I could give her a thank-you hug. She came running and we hugged, both in appreciation for different, but equally important reasons. This is also what Love tastes like and feels like.
****

Can you think of a similar event that you can choose to perceive as a gift of Love?

_____

_____

_____

_____

_____

_____

_____

_____

_____

_____

_____

_____

_____

_____

December 25

"Love is always patient and kind; it is never jealous, love is never boastful or conceited; it is never rude or selfish; it does not take offense, and it is not resentful. Love takes no pleasure in other people's sins but delights in the truth; it is always ready to excuse, to trust, to hope, and to endure whatever comes. Love does not come to an end." Bible

Binnie and Wanda L

When it was still not certain I would live, Binnie and Wanda came to visit. They brought me a prayer pillow entitled, "I Said A Prayer For You Today." The prayer goes on with:

> "I said a prayer for you today; And know God must have heard; I felt the answer in my heart; Although He spoke no word; I didn't ask for wealth or fame; I knew you wouldn't mind; I asked Him to send treasures; Of a far more lasting kind; I asked that He'd be near you; At the start of each new day; To grant you health and blessings; And friends to share your way; I asked for happiness for you; In all things great and small; But it was for His loving care; I prayed the most of all."

What can I add to this? I believe the pillow says it all. This is what Love does and says.

****

Can you think of a similar event that you can choose to perceive as a gift of Love?

_____

_____

_____

_____

_____

_____

_____

_____

_____

_____

_____

_____

_____

_____

December 26
"Nothing makes one feel so strong as a call for help." Pope Paul VI

Ricky MacI

When part of the family was travelling for 10 weeks with one of their stops being Hawaii, Aunt Ricky also wanted to go. Her husband did not want to travel all that way, so she asked me if I would go to be her companion. What a request! Did I? Did I! Of course, I did! She went with the rest of the travelling members a week before I went; however, she and I came home together. We had a fabulous time, laughed a lot, peed by the side of the mountain roads on the way to Hana, lost sunglasses because they slid off the hood of the car on that mountain road while stopped, found them again, ate wonderful food, met great people, swam in warm water, walked on black sandy beaches. It was idyllic. She trusted me that I would look after her on her one and only major vacation trip halfway around the world. This is what Love asks.

****

Can you think of a similar event that you can choose to perceive as a gift of Love?

_____

_____

_____

_____

_____

_____

_____

_____

_____

_____

_____

_____

_____

_____

December 27

"Unconditional love is the most powerful stimulant to the immune system." Bernie Siegal

Karen W

When I was 'only five!' which I would say after my near death experience to mark my new existence by present years, I happened to be in the near-by town just before Spring clean-up. The things that were thrown out by the students leaving for the year and not taking their apartment or house furniture with them was in large piles at curbside waiting to be picked up by the waste management trucks. I saw a double bed box spring and immediately thought, "Aha, that would make a great raised garden 'bed' in which to grow vegetables." My friend Karen happened to visit unexpectedly and I asked her to come with me to reclaim some of the thrown-out, but reuseable, items for our own recycling. She was willing. I then borrowed my father's half-ton truck and off we went. We brought the box spring home along with some other pieces of furniture. Karen helped me position the repurposed raised garden bed frame on the back lawn to be used for vegetable-growing. This is what spontaneous acts of Love looks like, too.

****

Can you think of a similar event that you can choose to perceive as a gift of Love?

December 28
"My first thoughts are that I should not let people down, that I should support them and love them." Princess of Wales Diana

Richard G

I got this lovely email one day. It said that Richard had been over to the ocean shore to my property and that he saw this wonderful piece of driftwood there. He dragged it up off the shore and planted it on my property as a piece of art. This is what Love looks like, too.
****

Can you think of a similar event that you can choose to perceive as a gift of Love?

_____

_____

_____

_____

_____

_____

_____

_____

_____

_____

_____

_____

_____

_____

_____

_____

_____

December 29

"Work like you don't need the money, love like you've never been hurt and dance like nobody's watching." Author Unknown

Barbie G

While recuperating with the shattered leg, many people came and went with soothing words, home-made foodstuffs, cards, funny stories, but no one offered to wash my back or massage my feet – only Barbie. Barbie would come and make meals, do laundry, change my bed, and, especially, she would help me into the bathtub and onto the special seat, she would get the water temperature right, she would lather all the parts of my body that I couldn't reach, and then she would help me out of the bathtub, and she would towel me down and then cut my toenails and massage my feet and legs with oils, all the while talking about how much she loved helping others. Her ministrations were so unbelievably kind and gentle and caring. She treated me to this special kind of Loving when I really needed it.

****

Can you think of a similar event that you can choose to perceive as a gift of Love?

_____

_____

_____

_____

_____

_____

_____

_____

_____

_____

_____

_____

_____

December 30
"Our sorrows and wounds are healed only when we touch them with compassion."
Buddha

Jamie G

Whenever I came back into consciousness while lying on the gurney in the hallway of the Emergency Room, I would see my brother, Jamie, standing there. Sometimes he was just looking down at me, sometimes he was on his cell phone, but he was always there. He says Mom and Dad also came to stand by the gurney while I was there, but I don't remember seeing them. I lay on the gurney with my left leg shattered and at an odd angle for 2 days, 2 days while the hospital staff wondered if I was strong enough to withstand anesthesia and surgery. I really don't think the alternative was very viable. Whenever I was conscious, the pain was so enveloping that a nurse would come and give me an injection in my hip and I either threw up from being allergic to the drug or passed out again. Jamie can never know how comforting it was to have him there where I knew he was advocating for me as I was unable to do so for myself. Him standing on guard for me was a showering mountain of Love.

****

Can you think of a similar event that you can choose to perceive as a gift of Love?

_____

_____

_____

_____

_____

_____

_____

_____

_____

_____

_____

_____

_____

_____

December 31

"There can be no Security without Peace
There can be no Peace without Freedom
There can be no Freedom without Justice
There can be no Justice without Love."
Graffiti from a wall in Thailand

Myself

What have I learned in all this? That love is an infinite wave of particles, sometimes concrete in the physical, many times celestial in the ethereal. If we but slow down and really see, hear, touch, feel, sense, taste and intuit the well-meaning of absolutely every encounter we have, then, we can allow our souls to grow in compassion and we can learn to love with all our hearts and minds and souls without reservation. In order to do this, we must put away any emotion from the Fear bucket. We must. It is not an option. Only Love paves the way for us to learn about the lessons we came here to have. It's all about Love. It's only about Love. Love is all there is. This is what I have learned. Thank you. I love you, Patricia. And, it is so, and So, it is.

****

Can you think of a similar event that you can choose to perceive as a gift of Love?

_____

_____

_____

_____

_____

_____

_____

_____

_____

_____

_____

_____

_____

_____

Do you recognize and honour Love as it happens in your life? Every day? Every minute? Can you recognize Love in its vagaries and varieties and hues and shades: the colour, taste, smell, sound, sight of Love – or is it only a feeling that you recognize? It might surprise you to realize that we all want Love, talk about it, search for it, dream of it, yet, we so often fail to recognize it when we are graced with its presence. **THIS IS WHAT LOVE LOOKS LIKE, TOO** is a journal within a journal, a daily honouring of Love's grace. Each day has a real-life occurrence of Love experienced by the author to help the reader understand how big little acts of Love really are in our daily lives. Recognizing, honouring, and writing down the little acts of Love on a daily basis will help the reader to shift the perception from a position of doubt and fear to realize that most, in fact, probably, all, events have Love in them – the challenge is for each of us to take the time to recognize the gift and then to savour and honour it and take it into our hearts and lives.

ABOUT THE AUTHOR

Dr. Grover Dix was born and still lives in the Annapolis Valley of Nova Scotia, Canada. She has a B.A. in Psychology, a Bachelor of Education, and a Ph.D. in Holistic Life Counseling from the University of Sedona from where she also successfully obtained her metaphysical minister's designation.

Experiencing a near death experience, she was given the cosmic chance to choose whether to actively live or to passively continue to die. When she chose life, her total orientation and perception changed. She has accepted the responsibility to think and act and believe that her life's purpose here is to learn about the varieties and vagaries of Love and to share these with others by writing, teaching, 'planting seeds', and acting as a catalyst. She continues to learn about the metaphysical mysteries of life, sharing these understandings back out with others who may find them helpful. All is good, and so it is.

She can be reached at patdix46@gmail.com

Made in the USA
Charleston, SC
19 March 2015